1

MAURICE NIO
UNSEEN I SLIPPED AWAY

010 PUBLISHERS
Rotterdam 2004

CONTENTS >

SOVEREIGNTY & SINGULARITY >

One day, after her mother had scolded her for making silly animal noises, Laurie stopped speaking. She was four years old. 'Soon Laurie gave up bowel control. A while later began an ever more severe withdrawal from the world, which by the age of six had reached such proportions that for long time periods she seemed blind, deaf, and unable to move on her own. Most of the time she spent her days motionless, staying wherever she was put, sitting in a chair, on the floor, or on the toilet, until bodily moved by someone to some other place. The small remainder of her days she spent in an empty turning of magazine pages without looking at them, or in tearing them into the tiniest pieces.' Thus begins the story of Laurie in the book The Empty Fortress by Bruno Bettelheim. It tells of a girl whose budding personality was disrupted by misguided discipline. Her physical capacities dwindled, one by one, and within two years she had withdrawn into the secrecy of her own body.

The girl's mother brought the inert, apparently autistic child to a specialized institute. The team of caregivers patiently applied everything they knew to lure her back into the world. First Laurie had to learn to feed herself again, for she had become seriously anorectic. Little by little, crumb by crumb, raisin by raisin. She had to relearn the most basic human functions, but it was no good moulding her movements for her imitations would become meaningless and mechanical. A crucial moment was the recognition of her own faeces, for she had so far been unaware of the distinction between her excreta and herself. One day, the little, hard stools, which she let fall unregarded, lay among her wooden building blocks. She picked up both things, faeces and toy blocks, one by one, and played with them. After playing this game repeatedly for four days, she was beginning to show signs of awareness of her excreta. Not only was it dawning on her that she could do something and have control over it, but she began to realize that her faeces were no longer part of herself. They were disconnected from her identity, like the toy building blocks.

Gradually, Laurie rediscovered herself. She learned that she could have control over the various parts of her body and over things that were not part of her. She learnt too to make sounds again. Somewhere, deep in that extinguished childish spirit, a flame of life rekindled. But without that first crucial step, becoming conscious of the difference between the self and the nonself, it would have remained inert. Her excrement was the key by which she could learn, little by little, to reemerge as a person, as a sovereign individual.

The story of Laurie serves as a rough script for the development of personal sovereignty. It is an unpolished mirror of the relation between people and things. Thanks to the excreted product, that strange, dead thing, Laurie became someone instead of no-one. And the same applies to us all. Without the 'nonself' we would remain in an embryonic stage and be unable to release ourselves from a condition of inertia. The lifeless makes it possible for life to commence. Only that which stands outside the human being – the inhuman – can engender humanity. The thing is the trigger of living existence. Whether a stool, a painting or a car – everything we produce and with which we then engage helps boost our self-sovereignty. This implies that the 'nonself' is not some insignificant, simple object which, once having been produced, slavishly loiters around until picked up and used. No, it is a self-willed, ambiguous thing that covertly awaits the quickening of our consciousness. In the thing, there lies something vital, an invisible energy source, an inbuilt drive. The thing has been conceived and made in order to transmit that vitality to a person.

In principle, any thing could function as the spark of existence. Even now that the universe of 'the nonself' consists of a fabulous quantity of objects, signs and information, all components of this universe can function in the same way as Laurie's faeces. However, there are things that could be function better and more intensely than others; things that cannot be expressed in terms of money and thus are scarcely capable of being commercialized; things that have a specific, symbolic value and are difficult to decode; things that bear particular watermarks and cannot be duplicated; things that do not fit into a system and are hard to convert; things that are, to put it simply, singular.

Singular objects all have one hallmark in common: they are never unequivocal or completely rational. Rather, they are naked and veiled at the same time. They are simultaneously clear and vague, as though our powers of perception slide off them. The singular is both visible and invisible. That lucky sixpence, that stuffed pelican, that yellowing photo, that pop idol's shirt, that lock of hair... The singular can surface in any form, as a mass produced product or a unique object, but it will always be equivocal. Thanks to the pact with the subject, and the subject's equivocality, the singular object can never be substituted, exchanged, converted, duplicated or reproduced. And it is the singular object's unsubstitutability that ultimately makes the subject itself non-interchangeable and sovereign.

For that is what actually matters: the sovereignty of the subject. And this sovereignty can only be achieved by entering into a bond with the animate and inanimate; a bond which develops into an inexplicable worship, counter to every reason or rationality. To others, the singular object is almost certainly a worthless thing or a superstitious fetish. For yourself, however, its absence is unthinkable. The thing is after all not just any thing. It is the instigator of a blinding love; your true partner; something with which you have made a highly subjective but binding pact. The more loyal this pact, the greater the degree of sovereignty. That is why the interdependence of the singular and the sovereign is crucial. The power of things determines the power of consciousness.

However, as Bruno Bettelheim rightly remarks, the covert fear will always remain that 'if any part of what was self (stools) can become nonself, then all of self may become nonself and disappear.' If we are capable of discharging something, and then turn out to be capable of spawning more and more different things, won't the sovereign self totally dissolve in favour of the nonself and thereby degenerate into a gel-like formlessness? Why don't we just evaporate like snow in the sunshine? Isn't that quite simply the anxiety that bothers everyone in our present culture? Hasn't our sovereignty melted away under the onslaught of a galaxy of products and information? Isn't it true that the consumer is consumed by the overwhelming range of things on offer? And aren't we, like Laurie, all consequently softened into the consistency of a biscuit dunked in tea?

The present blackmail that dictates our permanent presence online only makes things more complex. If you aren't nowadays hooked up in some or other way to the global network, you count for nothing. You must be either a toddler or a fundamentalist. The pressure to remain instantly pluggable, accessible, downloadable and of course virus-free, is an unrelenting force. The Internet can therefore no longer be regarded as a virtual, liberal network in which the individual can play his own little game, but as a concrete, compelling order in which the tyranny of the availability of information has the upper hand. The network demands that everything is available and visible, whereas the principle of personal sovereignty relies on intractability and equivocality. Does that mean we have to stay offline to remain sovereign? No, for the network also has its blind corners, shadowy nooks where no backups can be made and where the sovereign self is more than manifest.

Remarkably, though, the extinction of sovereignty in the network era could be given an opposite interpretation. For isn't connection to the network an ironic or perhaps even a cynical act on the part of the individual – to surrender to the pressure to be present and visible precisely with the intention of being absent and invisible? Perhaps the network has the same unconscious function as away-from-it-all holiday formulas like Center Parcs which unashamedly aim at the production of absence. Perhaps, too, insofar as it is a producer of absence and a human excrescence, the network is not unlike the faeces of Laurie, a potential aid to cultivating the sovereignty of the self. Who knows?

Everyone can therefore recognized themselves to some extent in Laurie, in that little girl who somehow managed to extricate herself from her inert existence. We can all conceive and produce objects which have a high intensity, objects with a special, personal value: singular objects. The creative process concerned is not something hazy, but one in which shape is given in the most lucid way possible to the mysterious, the equivocal, the ambiguous and the reversible. And that is only possible if that shape is clear-cut and at the same time vague. Only then can there be any secret to it. Just as the sovereign exists by virtue of the singular, so the singular exists by virtue of the secret.

In producing a secret, technique plays an important part. You always need some engineering to give shape to the equivocal and ambiguous. The world of rationality, of technology, usually gets the blame for the downfall of the secretive dimension. In the hands of a civil servant or an army officer, technology is perhaps a weapon for destroying the symbolic, secretive order; but for someone who has to create something rather than analyse, archive or attack something, it is an instrument for producing secrets. Consider the 37 secrets 'hidden' in every Euro banknote, purely in order to prevent duplication, imitation and counterfeiting. These secrets are in principle visible, of course. But it is precisely that – the friction between what is visible and what is invisible – that is the essence of the singular. Besides, the loveliest secrets are public secrets.

Consider the flavouring of Coca-Cola, the quintessential public secret. The secret is long out, but the flavour somehow has never been perfectly imitated. Or take the example of the television painter, Bob Ross. How on earth is it possible that he makes every brushstroke clearly visible and even explains them in his ever-unctuous tones, yet the final result remains inimitable? Is that just a trick of the trade? Is it the same secret that such masters as Paganini, Houdini and Buster Keaton possessed? Is the real talent to lack talent but have an abundance of skill and virtuosity? As with the conjuror or politician, the illusion is based purely on technique. It seems to be done in a detached way, more or less as a matter of routine. Everything is visible to the eye but invisible to the mind. The secret lies in the public realm, in the dazzling spotlight of the network, in the zone where secrets cannot possibly stay secret.

Whether found, bought or constructed, a singular object always bears a visible secret within it in the form of a watermark or code. It is something that comes from outside and ingrains itself into the object; something that is not worth deciphering because it does not yield anything interesting; a more or less casual adjunct that cannot be described in aesthetic terms; something free and unasked for. A code is the opposite of a concept or theme. A code is neither compelling nor explicit. Concepts and themes, on the other hand, always clamour for attention. They are noisy. With codes, on the other hand, the silence of a faked scene predominates. We are in a theatre without an audience or applause, a world without a denouement.

There is nothing to explain, only a pact to be respected.

The embedding of a code in the design of a product – a book, a film, a meal, a building etc. – is a technique that anyone can use. The skill is in ensuring the thing that is thought up and produced is haunted by an alien chimera. Once the mental image has taken possession of the heart of the product without making its presence immediately obvious, the object has a secret, and is thus a singular object. As the songwriter Moby said, 'It's weird, maybe, but every song I write, I imagine this specific kind of person who is listening to it alone, always alone, sitting by himself or herself. I have written a song where I imagine it's being listened to by a woman who's just come home from a hard day's work and finally has a moment to herself. I've written a song where it's a student in Germany on a train, coming home from school for the holidays.'

By invoking the specific individual, Moby gives his songs the exact charge they need to become singular. The recall of a person can serve this purpose, but so can the picture of an animal, an impossible geometry, a certain smell, number or colour, or a shocking fact; as in the case of Laurie, whose discovery that her excreta are dead but that she is alive marked her moment of rebirth.

If the singular object is the trigger of existence, then its form is the filter between the code and the experience. The outward form makes the secret literally tangible. That outward form – liminal or crystalline, soft or hard, mental or mineral – has to be just as ambiguous as the singular object itself. The form is not an impervious shell or armour, for it must be porous to the code while retaining sufficient integrity not to let too much leak out. It is marvellous to zoom in onto the form and see how mystifying its surface is. At precisely the point where everything ought to resolve into absolute visibility, into pornographic clarity, all we see is a fog of details. The totality of details constitutes the object, yet manipulating them or revealing more of them will not yield a sharper picture.

The details fly in the face of the principle of clarity. This principle always aims, after all, to leave things for they are – without shadows, without a sting in the tail, without ambiguity. It is a craving for confirmation. Let's hope that the things won't withdraw into themselves, that they won't deviate from holy self-confirmation... It is this thirst for certainty that the details tend to subvert.

Details have just one goal: to externalize the code, and then immediately hide it again. That is why details are always black-and-white. They make the mystery tangible but not visible. And even if the details were capable of betraying the secret, that revelation would be fruitless. The watermarks of the singular are legible in the singular but there is no point in trying to read them. As the top model Kate Moss said, in a sly swipe at the press, '... the more visible they make me, the more invisible I become.'

THE SERENDIPITY OF MACHINES >

Friday, 20 August 1993, 13.30 hrs. The phone rings. It is Herr Gebeshuber. He works for Fichtner, a German firm of consulting engineers. He is calling to confirm who has been selected to design the new building for the waste treatment plant in Hengelo. 'Congratulations. You are our chosen architect. Can you give a presentation of your concept and a possible shape for the building? Seven working days from now?' 'Er... OK.'

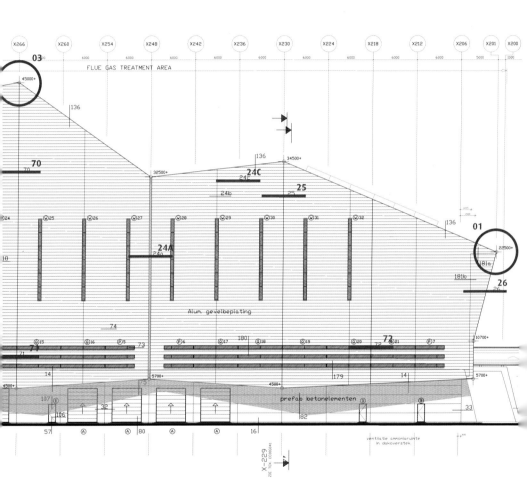

What do you do when someone commissions you to design a building for machines? That is to say, not a building for people and human activities, but a plant for transforming garbage into useful products, into energy and clean air? A building which has zero percent public functions? A building which is occupied by only the seven operatives responsible for keeping the incinerators going?

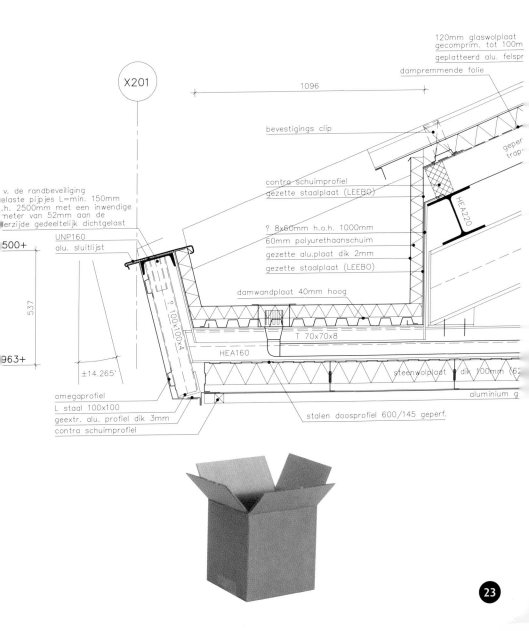

120mm glaswolplaat
gecomprim. tot 100m
geplatteerd alu. felspr
dampremmende folie

X201

1096

bevestigings clip

geper
trap

contra schuimprofiel
gezette staalplaat (LEEBO)

HEA220

v. de randbeveiliging
elaste pijpjes L=min. 150mm
.h. 2500mm met een inwendige
meter van 52mm aan de
erzijde gedeeltelijk dichtgelast

? 8x60mm h.o.h. 1000mm
60mm polyurethaanschuim
gezette alu.plaat dik 2mm
gezette staalplaat (LEEBO)

UNP160
alu. sluitlijst

500+

damwandplaat 40mm hoog

537

? 100x100x4

T 70x70x8

HEA160

963+

±14.265'

steenwolplaat dik 100mm (6

aluminium g

omegaprofiel
L staal 100x100
geextr. alu. profiel dik 3mm
contra schuimprofiel

stalen doosprofiel 600/145 geperf.

23

How many dreams and nightmares, how many books and films, are there about machines taking over the world? Many, very many. It's not all that surprising really. Humanity has always secretly hoped that some non-human force would rescue us from our human hegemony. Why not machines? The dream looms real here, in this vast interior populated by machines, in this Valhalla of steel sphinxes.

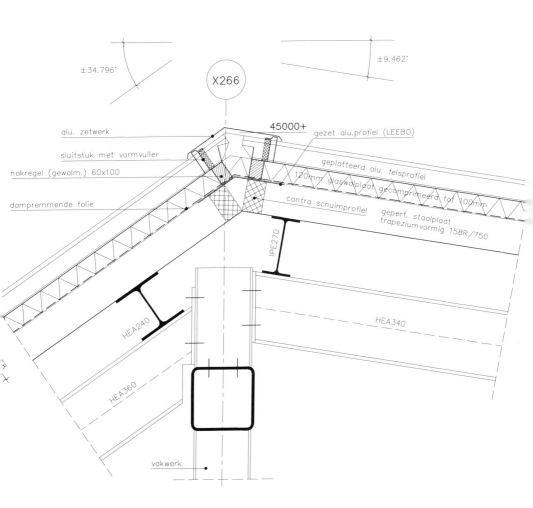

±34.796˙

X266

±9.462˙

alu. zetwerk

45000+

gezet alu.profiel (LEEBO)

sluitstuk met vormvuller

geplatteerd alu. felsprofiel

nokregel (gewolm.) 60x100

120mm glaswolplaat gecomprimeerd tot 100mm

contra schuimprofiel

dampremmende folie

geperf. staalplaat
trapeziumvormig 158R/750

IPE270

HEA240

HEA340

HEA360

vakwerk

In these halls (a word that barely does them justice) our sense of superiority evaporates. The plant is paramount here, not mankind. These spaces are not determined by human dimensions but by the size of the machinery, which is purchased on a basis of price and reliability. After all, these machines were selected and combined purely on the basis of functionality. Or weren't they?

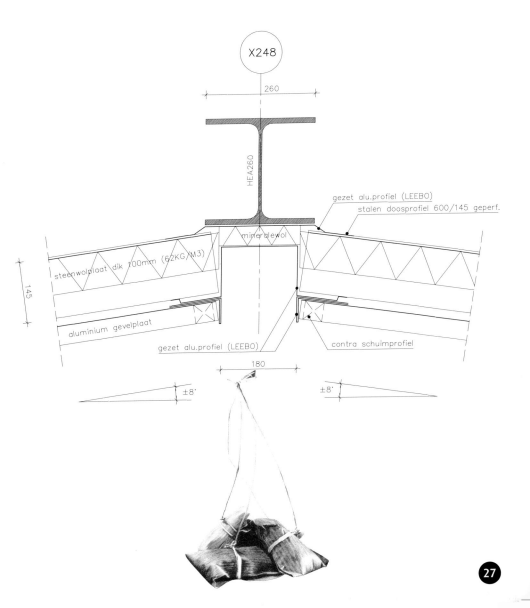

X248

260

HEA260

gezet alu.profiel (LEEBO)

stalen doosprofiel 600/145 geperf.

mineralewol

steenwolplaat dik 100mm (62KG/M3)

145

aluminium gevelplaat

gezet alu.profiel (LEEBO)

contra schuimprofiel

180

±8°   ±8°

27

You only have to look at photos like those above to get the impression of an ingress of machines, the triumphant cavalcade of a strange mechanical army whose makeup is incomprehensible to us. Or perhaps it is comprehensible only to those engineers who conceived it. But suppose that cortege of machines actually knows what formation it is supposed to take? Suppose they found one another through pure serendipity?

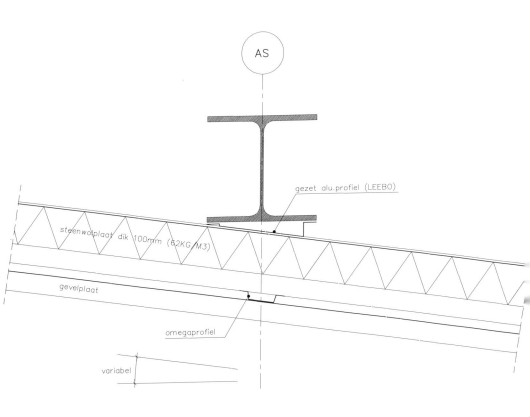

AS

gezet alu.profiel (LEEBO)

steenwolplaat dik 100mm (62KG/M3)

gevelplaat

omegaprofiel

variabel

Can machines be serendipitous? Can inanimate things be like sentient ones and discover something they were not looking for, through a combination faculties and fortune, intelligence and coincidence? In particular, could they devise this building? They have always known they belonged together, that they could only operate in this formation, and that there is hence no such thing as a coincidental formation.

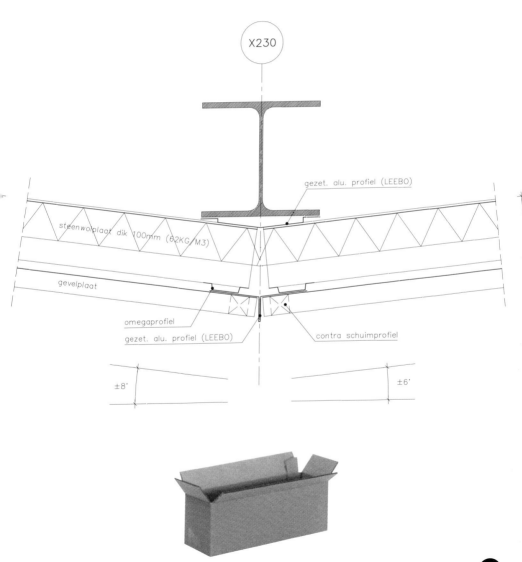

X230

gezet. alu. profiel (LEEBO)

steenwolplaat dik 100mm (62KG/M3)

gevelplaat

omegaprofiel

gezet. alu. profiel (LEEBO)

contra schuimprofiel

±8°

±6°

There is another reason why pure chance seems an unlikely explanation. Following our first proposal, the design of the building changed some ten times over five years, until finally, once everything had been worked out in detail, it showed a surprising similarity to that first little model of blue plastic foam. Since then I have no longer believed in chance. There has to be something behind what happens.

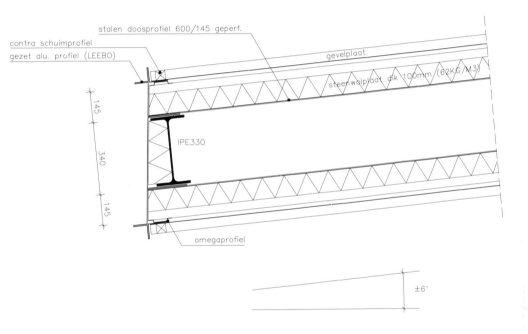

stalen doosprofiel 600/145 geperf.

contra schuimprofiel

gezet alu. profiel (LEEBO)

gevelplaat

steenwolplaat dik 100mm (62KG/M3)

145

340

145

IPE330

omegaprofiel

±6°

You get the rather worrying feeling that it wasn't you but the machines that decided the design. Probably that's true anyway. On the motorway, when you're surrounded on all sides by reckless road hogs, you sometimes wonder why there aren't more accidents. Maybe it's simply because the machines sense their position and destination and manage to avoid bumping into one another. That is the serendipity of machines.

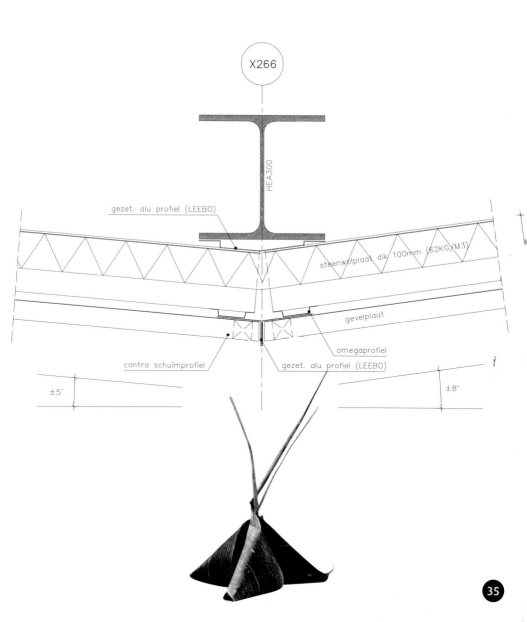

X266

HEA 300

gezet. alu profiel (LEEBO)

steenwolplaat dik 100mm (62KG/M3)

gevelplaat

omegaprofiel

contra schuimprofiel

gezet. alu profiel (LEEBO)

±5˚

±8˚

35

the aviTWENTE waste incineration plant in Hengelo, 1993-1997

The same suspicion steals up on you when you look at the
mannequins made by Bellmer. You recognize the human limbs
but their configuration is puzzling. Everything has been sewn
back together but the surgeon was obviously distracted during
the operation. The disturbing thing about the result is that you
can't help wondering 'why not?' What is wrong with its shape?
Is the shape of our own bodies really all that inevitable?

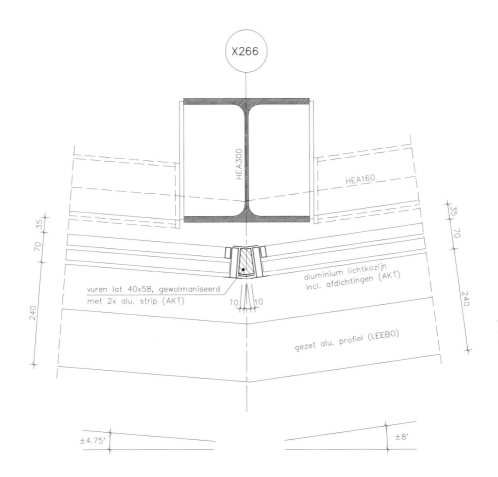

X266

HEA300

HEA160

35
70

240

vuren lat 40x58, gewolmaniseerd
met 2x alu. strip (AKT)

10   10

aluminium lichtkozijn
incl. afdichtingen (AKT)

gezet alu. profiel (LEEBO)

35
70

240

±4.75°   ±8°

The same question could be applied to this building. Why not? Is there any good reason why the components of the plant shouldn't appear in this particular formation? Despite all the interim changes, is this the 'right' shape for the building? A shape determined by the dimensions of the machinery. A form thought up by machines. But a question that always lurks in the background is 'why not?'

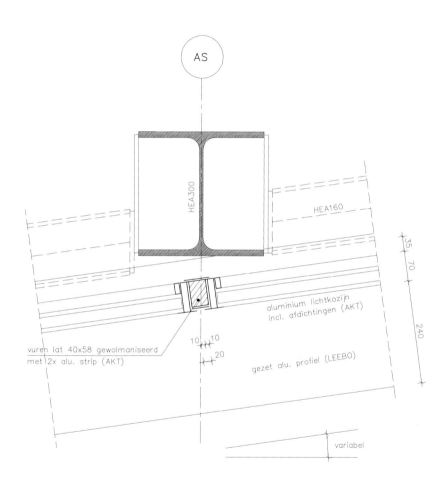

AS

HEA300

HEA160

35

70

240

aluminium lichtkozijn
incl. afdichtingen (AKT)

vuren lat 40x58 gewolmaniseerd
met 2x alu. strip (AKT)

10   10
20

gezet alu. profiel (LEEBO)

variabel

Perhaps that's the difference between identity and sovereignty.
Identity is simply based on potential recognition, but
sovereignty may consist of a mix of the familiar and the
uncanny. You can't focus your thoughts on a sovereign form. It is
too heavily determined by non-human forces to allow that.
Every human impulse towards recognition is defeated by that
inhuman ambiguity.

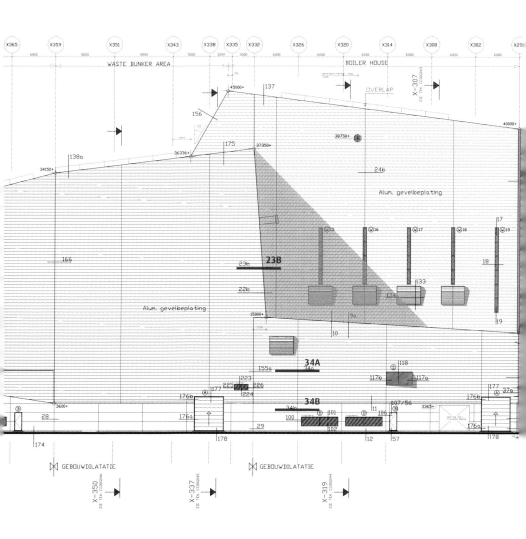

The opposite to identity is not genericness. As long as identity is regarded as a unit of being and the generic as a totality without being, they will always remain locked in an academic mock battle. Their contrived opposition is destructive to the extent that it fixes, stabilizes, homogenizes, aesthetizes and vitiates the relation between subject and object or between the person and the thing.

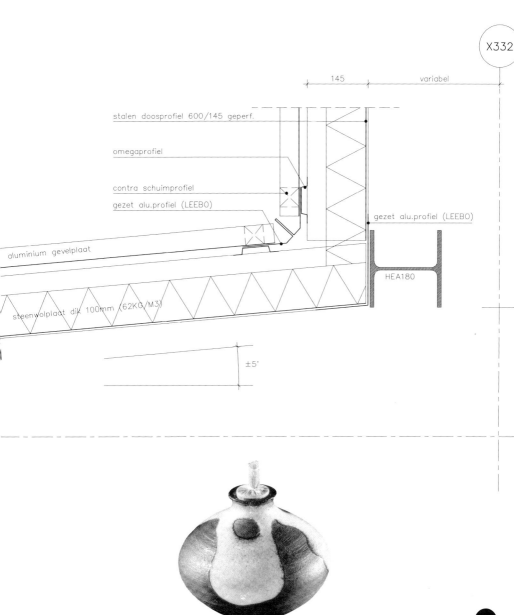

X332

145   variabel

stalen doosprofiel 600/145 geperf.

omegaprofiel

contra schuimprofiel

gezet alu.profiel (LEEBO)

gezet alu.profiel (LEEBO)

aluminium gevelplaat

HEA180

steenwolplaat dik 100mm (62KG/M3)

±5˚

The opposite to identity is not genericness but sovereignty. Is it possible to sidestep the contract between wholeness and totality, and to speak of a pact between the sovereign and the singular? About a pact between people and things? About a codified relationship which is indeed ambiguous? About the relation between the residents of Hengelo and their eccentric 'cathedral', dedicated to their own waste matter?

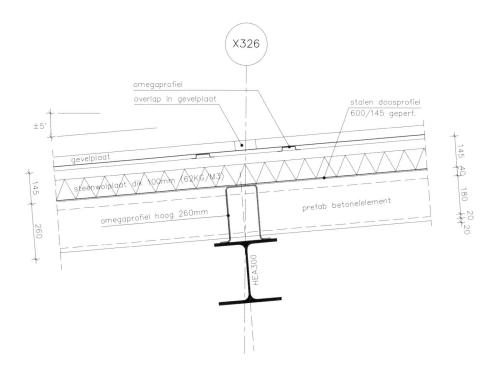

the aviTWENTE waste incineration plant in Hengelo, 1993-1997

The problematic but also splendid thing about complex tasks of this kind is that nobody possesses an overview of the entirety of the activities, neither during preparation nor during construction. This makes designing something like surfing on the breakers of a wild, uncontrollable flight from subcontractors, consultants and project leaders. The trick is to extract the maximum benefit from all the misunderstandings en route.

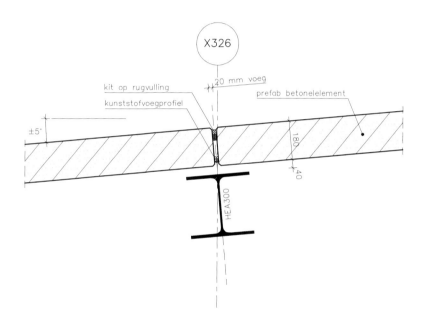

X326

20 mm voeg

kit op rugvulling

kunststofvoegprofiel

prefab betonelelement

±5°

180

40

HEA300

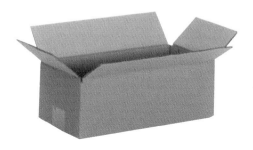

You do not have control over this building; fortunately so, you may think in a rash moment. After all, what is interesting about a 'successful' building? Nobody works for sake of the beatific look with which those project managers gaze upon their perfectly controlled planning, budget and quality charts. Complete control is impossible, thank heaven, in a large industrial construction project like this one.

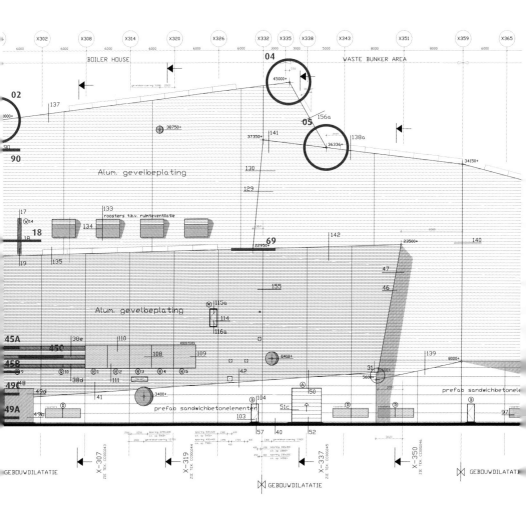

The only way it can happen is for all kinds of things to go wrong. The figures alone demonstrate this. As the project director Ad van Deursen said, 'Just bear in mind that in the last 5 years over 3 thousand people have worked on the project, that these people consulted with one another some 1.5 million times in 8 different languages, and that a misunderstanding arose in 5 percent of instances (75 thousand times)...

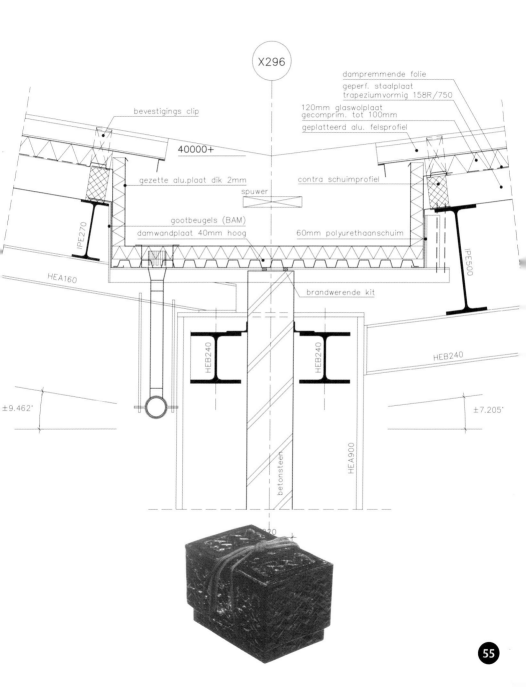

X296

dampremmende folie
geperf. staalplaat
trapeziumvormig 158R/750

bevestigings clip

120mm glaswolplaat
gecomprim. tot 100mm

geplatteerd alu. felsprofiel

40000+

gezette alu.plaat dik 2mm

contra schuimprofiel

spuwer

IPE270

gootbeugels (BAM)

damwandplaat 40mm hoog

60mm polyurethaanschuim

IPE500

HEA160

brandwerende kit

HEB240

HEB240

HEB240

±9.462˙

±7.205˙

HEA900

betonsteen

'... and that I myself travelled round the world 5 times, and that I was stuck in a traffic queue 194 times; and that about 16 thousand drawings had to be prepared, and all these drawings had to be changed time and time again; that over twelve hundred contracts were signed (although only 1 of them led to a lawsuit); that I moved house 7 times, and that power cuts occurred on 12 different occasions...

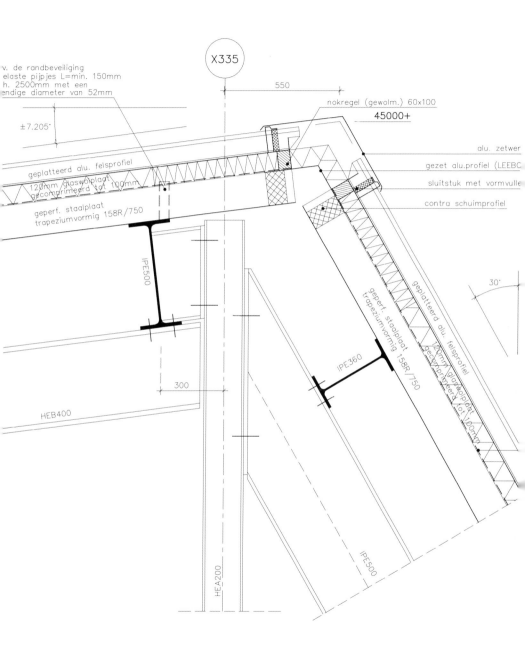

v. de randbeveiliging
elaste pijpjes L=min. 150mm
h. 2500mm met een
endige diameter van 52mm

X335

550

nokregel (gewolm.) 60x100

45000+

±7.205'

alu. zetwer

geplatteerd alu. felsprofiel

gezet alu.profiel (LEEBC

120mm glaswolplaat
gecomprimeerd tot 100mm

sluitstuk met vormvulle

contra schuimprofiel

geperf. staalplaat
trapeziumvormig 158R/750

IPE500

30'

geperf. staalplaat
trapeziumvormig 158R/750

geplatteerd alu. felsprofiel

120mm glaswolplaat
gecomprimeerd tot 100mm

IPE360

300

HEB400

HEA200

IPE500

'... that the garbage processing plant was eventually made up of 30 thousand separate components, hauled from 18 different countries by drivers who sometimes went to bed too early and sometimes too late; that we had 1 fire, and we celebrated the birth of 21 babies, including 2 grandchildren.' Is that what people mean by the law of averages? More than that, it's the law of the big project.

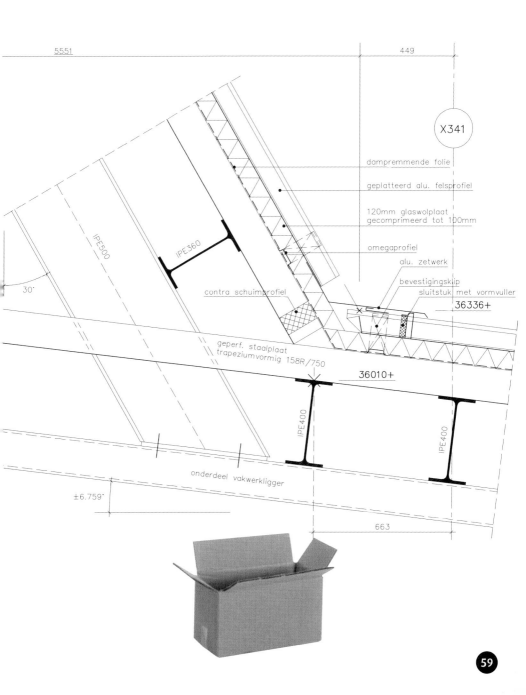

A large project imposes its own laws. They are the laws of a unique object. You can submit to them or not. Every theatre director, orchestral conductor or architect has difficulty capitulating to the blind laws of projects of this kind. The idea of autonomy has always been a ballast designers have had to carry. Not until you submit to the laws of the object can the sovereignty of the subject be established.

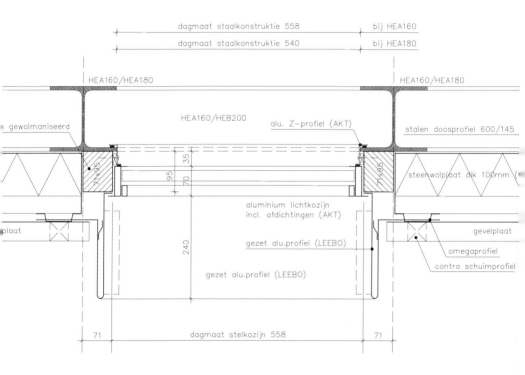

dagmaat staalkonstruktie 558   bij HEA160

dagmaat staalkonstruktie 540   bij HEA180

HEA160/HEA180   HEA160/HEA180

gewolmaniseerd

HEA160/HEB200   alu. Z-profiel (AKT)   stalen doosprofiel 600/145

35

95

70

71x95

71x95

steenwolplaat dik 100mm

aluminium lichtkozijn
incl. afdichtingen (AKT)

plaat   gevelplaat

240

gezet alu.profiel (LEEBO)

omegaprofiel

contra schuimprofiel

gezet alu.profiel (LEEBO)

71   dagmaat stelkozijn 558   71

During the opening, the councillor for spatial planning called, 'When this plant is written off in twenty years' time, it will have to be turned into a hotel.' My brain cells run amuck: guests sleeping in the furnace, a couple enjoying breakfast between electrostatic filters, an old gentleman taking a morning dip in the tank of potentiated water, toddlers playing on the conveyor belts amid the slag heaps...

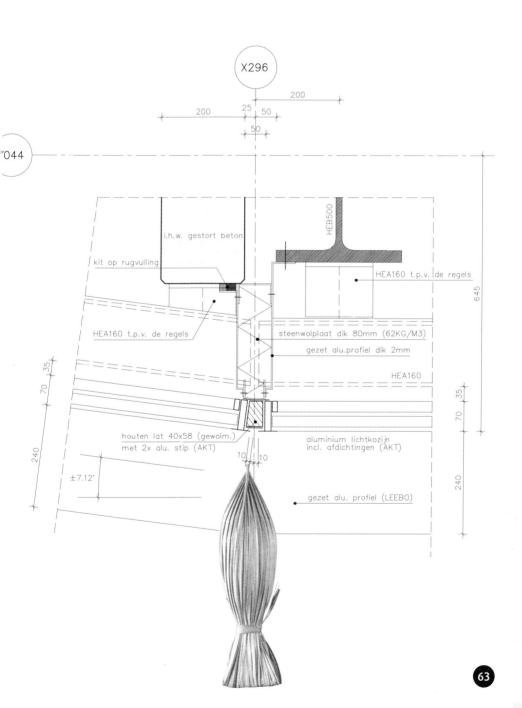

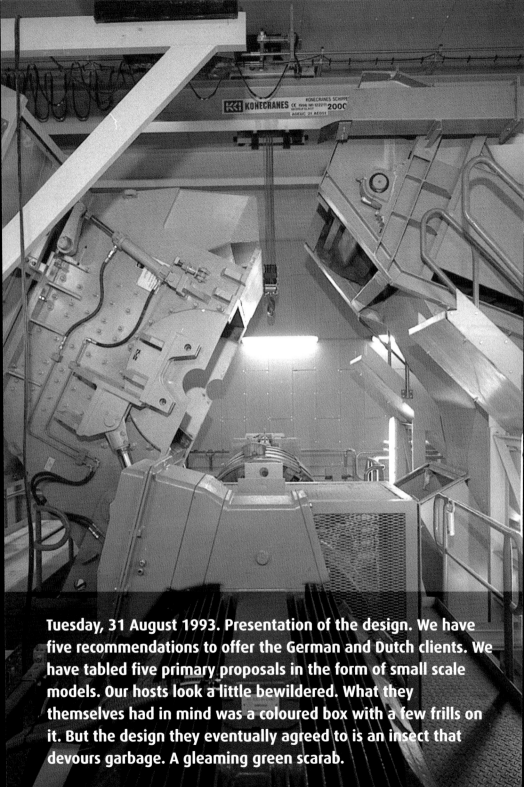

Tuesday, 31 August 1993. Presentation of the design. We have five recommendations to offer the German and Dutch clients. We have tabled five primary proposals in the form of small scale models. Our hosts look a little bewildered. What they themselves had in mind was a coloured box with a few frills on it. But the design they eventually agreed to is an insect that devours garbage. A gleaming green scarab.

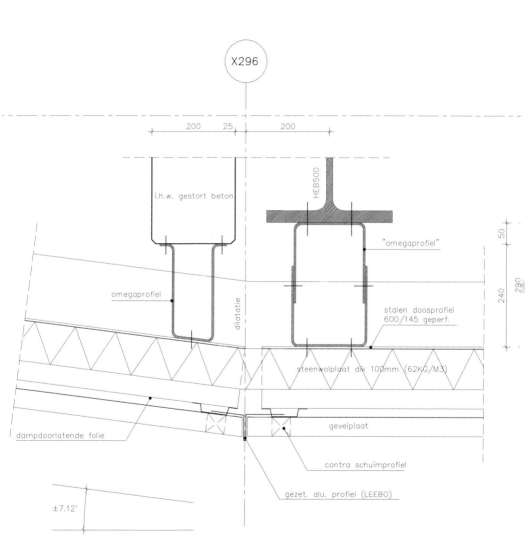

X296

200   25   200

i.h.w. gestort beton

HEB500

50

290

240

"omegaprofiel"

omegaprofiel

dilatatie

stalen doosprofiel
600/145 geperf.

steenwolplaat dik 100mm (62KG/M3)

gevelplaat

dampdoorlatende folie

contra schuimprofiel

gezet. alu. profiel (LEEBO)

±7.12'

65

The building has acquired the external features of the garbage dumps outside and the properties of the invisible incineration and purification process. It forms a filter between the rude landscape on the edge of Hengelo and the advanced equipment inside the plant. It functions as the interface between the external and internal landscape, between the unwieldy and the subtle technology, between the old and new ecology.

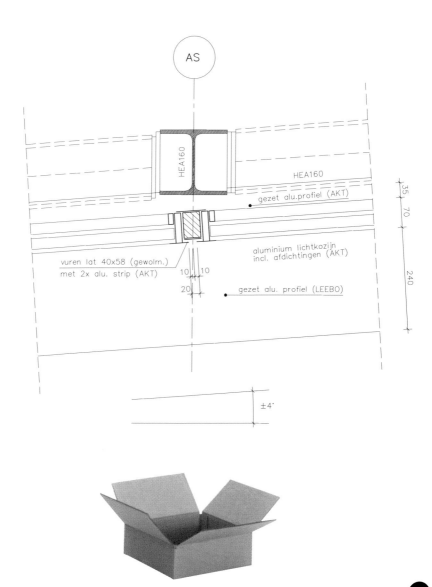

the aviTWENTE waste incineration plant in Hengelo, 1993-1997

As a designer, you always nurture the vain hope that the construction process for a huge, complex project like this can be a self-organizing system: you issue a set of game rules and trust that those 3,000 workers will make a nice job of it. However, in the course of five years it is inevitable that this hope will be dashed. Unlike Nature's self-regulating organisms, people always make a mess of it.

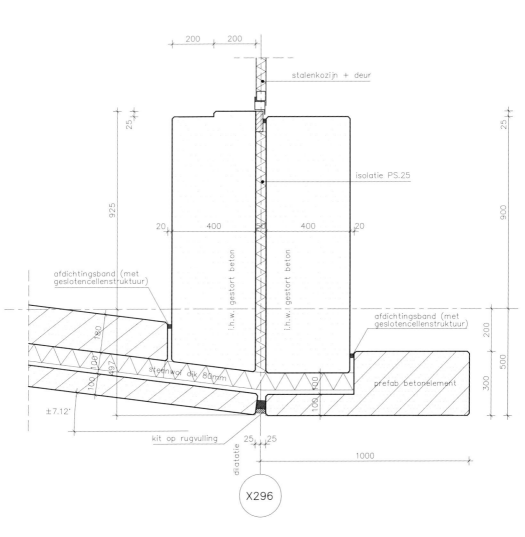

stalenkozijn + deur

isolatie PS.25

afdichtingsband (met
geslotencellenstruktuur)

afdichtingsband (met
geslotencellenstruktuur)

i.h.w. gestort beton

prefab betonelement

steenwol dik 80mm

kit op rugvulling

dilatatie

X296

So what is the architect's role? What is his position with regard to the innumerable technical wizards and civil engineers responsible for various parts of the plant? Is the architect responsible for the coherence and the logic of the whole project? Is the architect supposed to play at being a policeman, to guard the code, to direct the cultural and thus unrationalizable part of the totality?

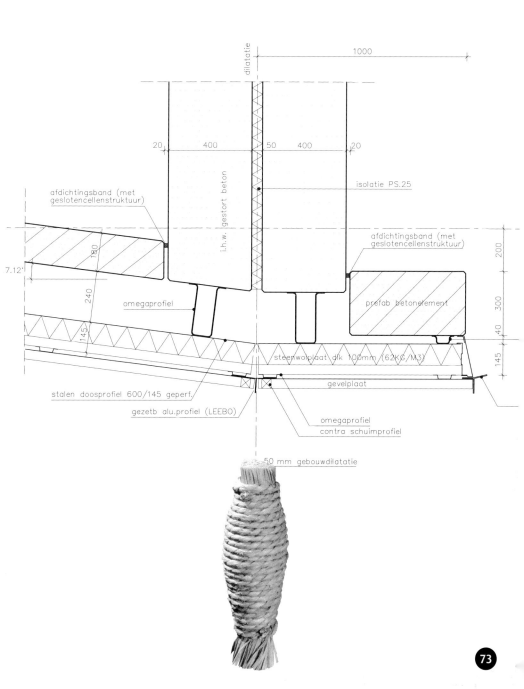

The architect's position here is not an enviable one. Fortunately, nobody knows the solution. Nobody knows what a waste incineration plant is supposed to be like, what the final dimensions will be of the machinery that dictates the form of the building. Nobody can predict how often the machinery and hence the design of the building will have to undergo modification during the design process.

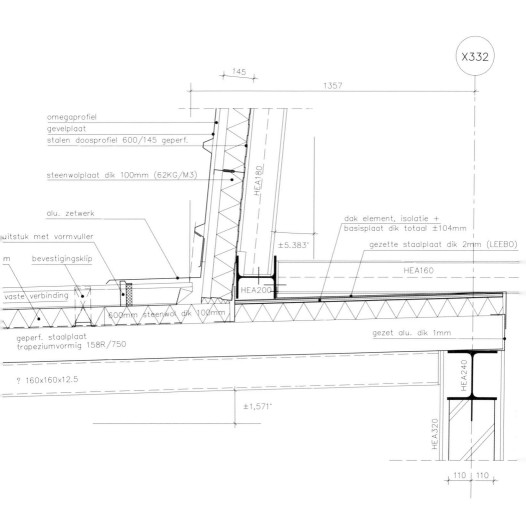

X332

145

1357

omegaprofiel
gevelplaat
stalen doosprofiel 600/145 geperf.

steenwolplaat dik 100mm (62KG/M3)

HEA180

alu. zetwerk

dak element, isolatie +
basisplaat dik totaal ±104mm

uitstuk met vormvuller

±5.383˙

gezette staalplaat dik 2mm (LEEBO)

m   bevestigingsklip

HEA160

vaste verbinding

HEA200

HEA240

600mm steenwol dik 100mm

geperf. staalplaat
trapeziumvormig 158R/750

gezet alu. dik 1mm

? 160x160x12.5

±1,571˙

HEA320

110 | 110

The architect has to devise a stratagem, an ingenious trick that will keep him going for five years. It must be proof against all the prosaic, short-term technical and functional demands. It must render all the technical preconditions into something ambiguous. It must be as tough as rocks and as clear as crystal. It must be vague and formless. It must be a stratagem like a sacred animal, like the Trojan Horse. An animal which is a code.

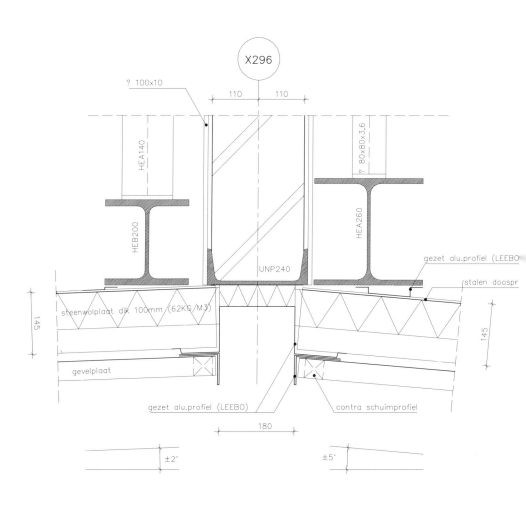

X296

? 100×10

110   110

HEA140

? 80×80×3,6

HEA260

HEB200

UNP240

gezet alu.profiel (LEEBO

stalen doospr

145

steenwolplaat dik 100mm (62KG/M3)

145

gevelplaat

gezet alu.profiel (LEEBO)   contra schuimprofiel

180

±2°   ±5°

Taking a closer view, the two independently functioning
incineration processes accomplish a digestion process. Both lines
have to be capable of incinerating 230,000 tons of waste per
annum and cleaning the emitted flue gas. The digestion process
is similar to that of a living thing. So why not propose a building
in the form of an insect, a gleaming, metallic dung beetle with
machine-like features? A green monster?

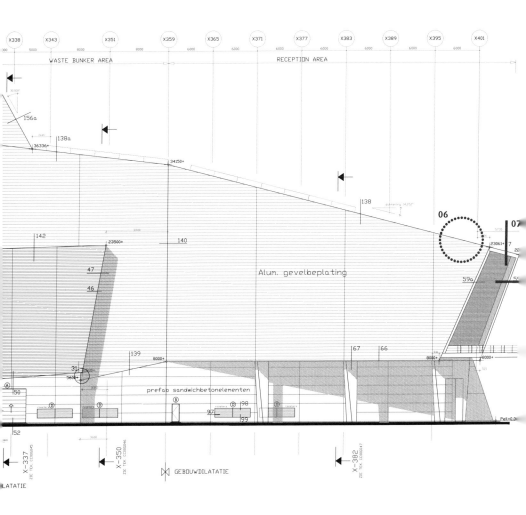

the aviTWENTE waste incineration plant in Hengelo, 1993-1997

07.08.01 15:31

Kamera 05 ONTVANGST HAL.

MONITOR 2

Waste Crane Cabin. The smallest space is half cantilevered above the abysmal stench of the bunker. It does not offer a view of the surroundings, but of garbage and the sky. It is manned day and night, and its form is dictated by impossibly strict ergonomic requirements. What must it be like sitting here, grubbing around in other people's garbage at two in the morning, trying to keep your concentration despite the moonlight?

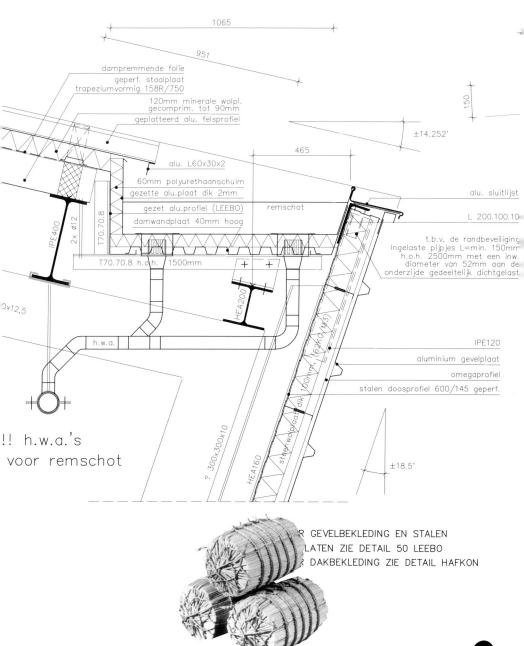

1065

951

dampremmende folie
geperf. staalplaat
trapeziumvormig 158R/750

120mm minerale wolpl.
gecomprim. tot 90mm
geplatteerd alu. felsprofiel

150

±14.252˙

465

alu. L60x30x2

60mm polyurethaanschuim
gezette alu.plaat dik 2mm
gezet alu.profiel (LEEBO)   remschot
damwandplaat 40mm hoog

T70.70.8 h.o.h. 1500mm

IPE400   2x ø12   T70.70.8

HEA200

h.w.a.

0x12,5

!! h.w.a.'s
voor remschot

? 300x300x10   HEA160   steenwolplaat dik 100mm. (62KG/M3)

alu. sluitlijst

L 200.100.10

t.b.v. de randbeveiliging
Ingelaste pijpjes L=min. 150mm
h.o.h. 2500mm met een inw.
diameter van 52mm aan de
onderzijde gedeeltelijk dichtgelast

IPE120

aluminium gevelplaat

omegaprofiel

stalen doosprofiel 600/145 geperf.

±18.5˙

R GEVELBEKLEDING EN STALEN
LATEN ZIE DETAIL 50 LEEBO
R DAKBEKLEDING ZIE DETAIL HAFKON

'The normal line of sight (optimal work posture) is about 15° below a horizontal. The optimal visual field is between the horizontal and 30° (zone A, comfort limit) below. A 'normal' work area is limited by the horizontal and 55° below (which is just above the knees; zone B). Incidentally a person could look downwards between his legs; this area is limited by the edge of the chair or the window at 71° (zone C)...'

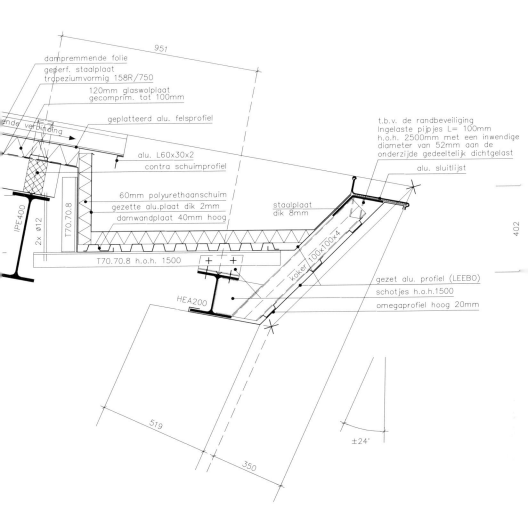

dampremmende folie
geperf. staalplaat
trapeziumvormig 158R/750

120mm glaswolplaat
gecomprim. tot 100mm

geplatteerd alu. felsprofiel

ande verbinding

alu. L60x30x2
contra schuimprofiel

60mm polyurethaanschuim
gezette alu.plaat dik 2mm
damwandplaat 40mm hoog

T70.70.8 h.o.h. 1500

HEA200

IPE400

2x ø12

T70.70.8

951

staalplaat
dik 8mm

koker 100x100x4

t.b.v. de randbeveiliging
Ingelaste pijpjes L= 100mm
h.o.h. 2500mm met een inwendige
diameter van 52mm aan de
onderzijde gedeeltelijk dichtgelast

alu. sluitlijst

gezet alu. profiel (LEEBO)
schotjes h.o.h.1500
omegaprofiel hoog 20mm

402

519

350

±24°

85

'... Sidewards, while leaning a bit over the arm rest, enables looking downwards to approximately 80° (not in figure 3). Optimal position for auxiliary information display (monitor) is approximately 10° above the horizontal (zone D). In a horizontal plane the optimal visual field is about 60° wide (without moving the head).' From Ergonomic Considerations, Waste Crane Cabin – a hallucinogenic set of functional requirements.

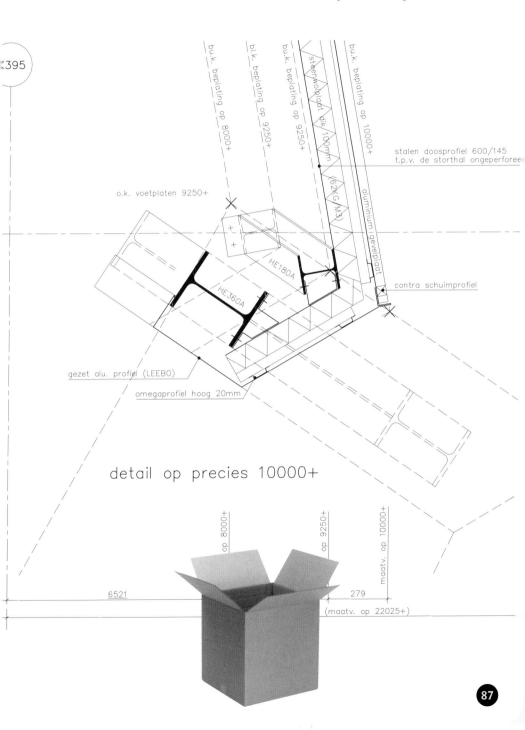

395

bu.k. beplating op 8000+

bi.k. beplating op 9250+

bu.k. beplating op 9250+

steenwolplaat dik 100mm

(62KG/M3)

bu.k. beplating op 10000+

aluminium gevelplaat

stalen doosprofiel 600/145
t.p.v. de storthal ongeperforee

o.k. voetplaten 9250+

contra schuimprofiel

HE180A

HE360A

gezet alu. profiel (LEEBO)

omegaprofiel hoog 20mm

detail op precies 10000+

op 8000+

op 9250+

maatv. op 10000+

6521

279

(maatv. op 22025+)

Defining this small space probably cost as much effort as the rest of the building put together. But even furnishings like the desk for the weighing station supervisor took years of design effort. The same applies to all the specialized furnishings, which sometimes have to be manned 24 hours a day. So we feel some sardonic pleasure and restrained pride in telling people we were even responsible for choosing the toilet roll holders.

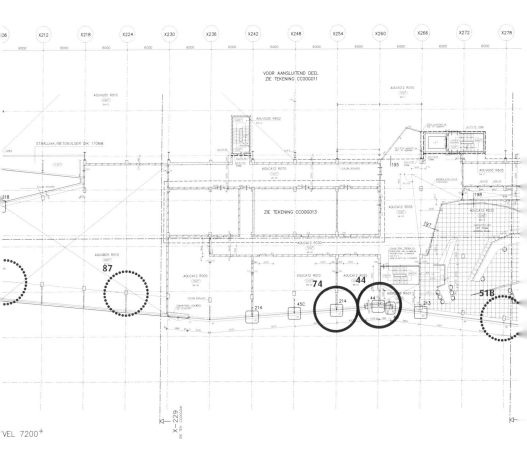

VEL 7200$^+$

The passion for control is a sin against the code. Everything in this design is under control, not only the secondary buildings around the main building, but also the detailing, the colour of the machines, the layout of the grounds and the numerous items of specialized furniture that swarm around the building like little insects. As architects, to what extent can we ignore the formation of machines and interpret the code differently?

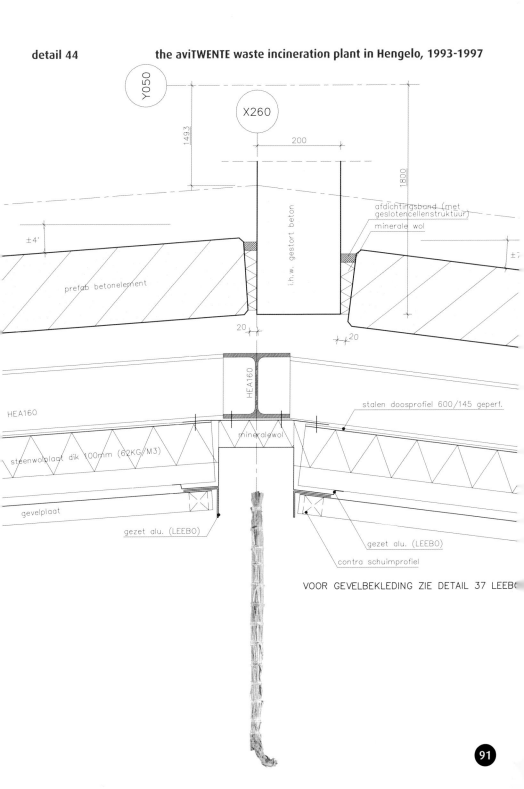

Y050

X260

1493

200

1800

i.h.w. gestort beton

afdichtingsband (met geslotencellenstruktuur)

minerale wol

±4°

prefab betonelement

±7

20

20

HEA160

stalen doosprofiel 600/145 geperf.

HEA160

mineralewol

steenwolplaat dik 100mm (62KG/M3)

gevelplaat

gezet alu. (LEEBO)

gezet alu. (LEEBO)

contra schuimprofiel

VOOR GEVELBEKLEDING ZIE DETAIL 37 LEEBO

Perhaps the quirky angular folds in the facade are the building's
finest feature. The projecting and reentrant angles are the
anchor points of a broken line that skirts the footprints of the
machines. This is the line that has changed time and time again
during the last five years, and is now fixed by the building itself.
But fixed is a misleading word. It is the line that animates the
building, that mentally sets the building in motion.

the aviTWENTE waste incineration plant in Hengelo, 1993-1997

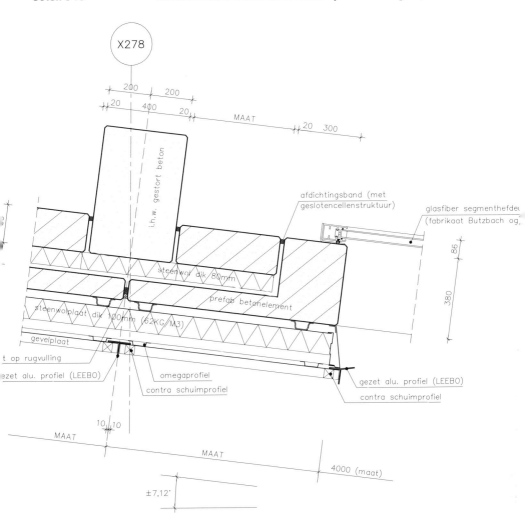

X278

200   200
20   400   20
MAAT
20   300

i.h.w. gestort beton

afdichtingsband (met
geslotencellenstruktuur)

glasfiber segmenthefde(
(fabrikaat Butzbach og,

86

steenwol dik 80mm

prefab betonelement

380

steenwolplaat dik 100mm (62KG/M3)

gevelplaat

t op rugvulling

ezet alu. profiel (LEEBO)

omegaprofiel

contra schuimprofiel

gezet alu. profiel (LEEBO)

contra schuimprofiel

10 10
MAAT

MAAT

4000 (maat)

±7,12·

This broken line actually forms a second horizon. Where garbage heaps once determined the horizon, the waste processing plant dictates a new one. It is no longer a horizon between heaven and earth, but one between cleanliness and dirt, between the past and the future of waste. This plant may well be a precursor of a world without residues, without leftovers, without surpluses.

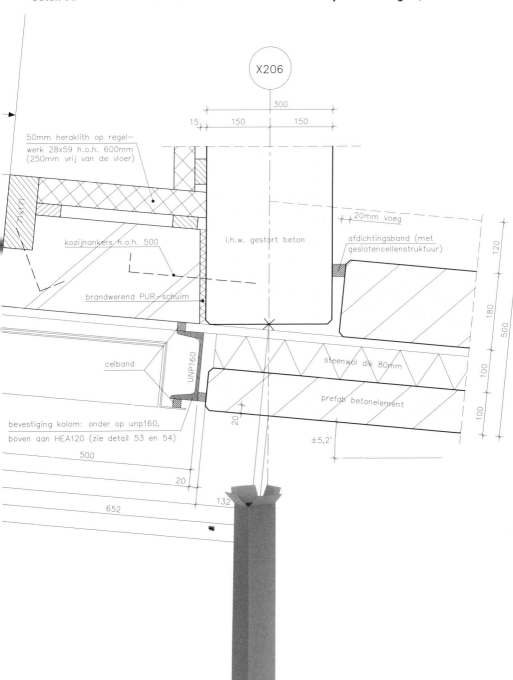

X206

300

15 · 150 · 150

50mm heraklith op regel—
werk 28x59 h.o.h. 600mm
(250mm vrij van de vloer)

kozijnankers h.o.h. 500

i.h.w. gestort beton

20mm voeg

afdichtingsband (met
geslotencellenstruktuur)

120

brandwerend PUR—schuim

180

500

celband

UNP160

steenwol dik 80mm

100

prefab betonelement

100

bevestiging kolom: onder op unp160,
boven aan HEA120 (zie detail 53 en 54)

±5,2˚

500

20

20

132

652

The natural illumination in the interior is as pleasing as the angles. It's wonderful how the long, horizontal slits just above the floor at the 7.2 metre level set the machinery afloat. This light source, plus the numerous roof lights, converts the interior into a theatre; a stage setting for machines. Since you usually walk around here in the company of only a few other people, it gives the feeling of an intimate surrealistic performance.

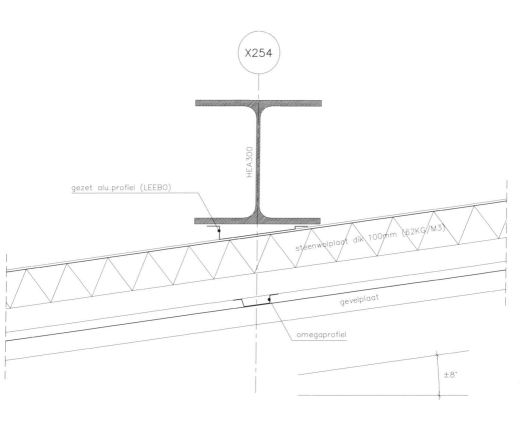

X254

HEA 300

gezet alu.profiel (LEEBO)

steenwolplaat dik 100mm (62KG/M3)

gevelplaat

omegaprofiel

±8°

A farmer working in the vicinity of the plant is pleased that the building is lit up so generously at night. It means he has to spend less on lighting himself. Besides, he gets a free clip from *Close Encounters of the Third Kind* every night. A photo of him and his dog shows them in a cattle stall with the sparkling plant in the background. Behold, a willing submission to the hegemony of machines.

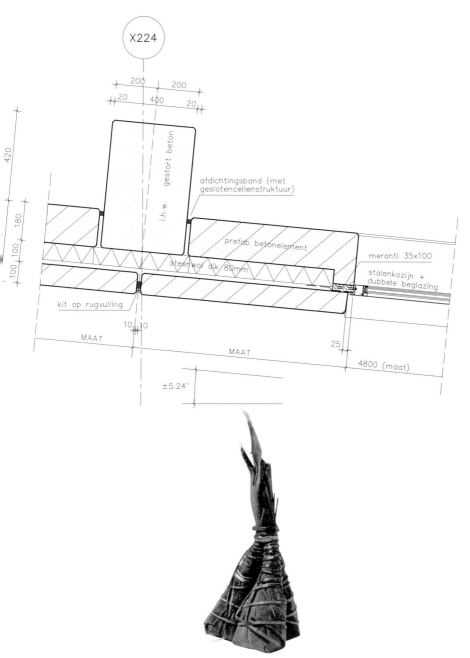

X224

200   200
20   400   20

420

180

100   100

i.h.w. gestort beton

afdichtingsband (met geslotencellenstruktuur)

prefab betonelement

steenwol dik 80mm

meranti 35x100

stalenkozijn +
dubbele beglazing

kit op rugvulling

10   10

MAAT

MAAT

25

4800 (maat)

180

100   100   380

±5.24*

THE CURVES OF COMMERCE >

We have always had a huge distaste for the colour white. Washbasins and toilet bowls in white are bad enough, but a white building or interior is something criminal. In China, white is the colour of mourning. The colour white stands for the absence of life, for the lack of pigmentation, for indifference towards 'the other', for a fear of dreams. White stands for a kind of insomnia.

furniture for The Village in Voorburg, 2001-2003

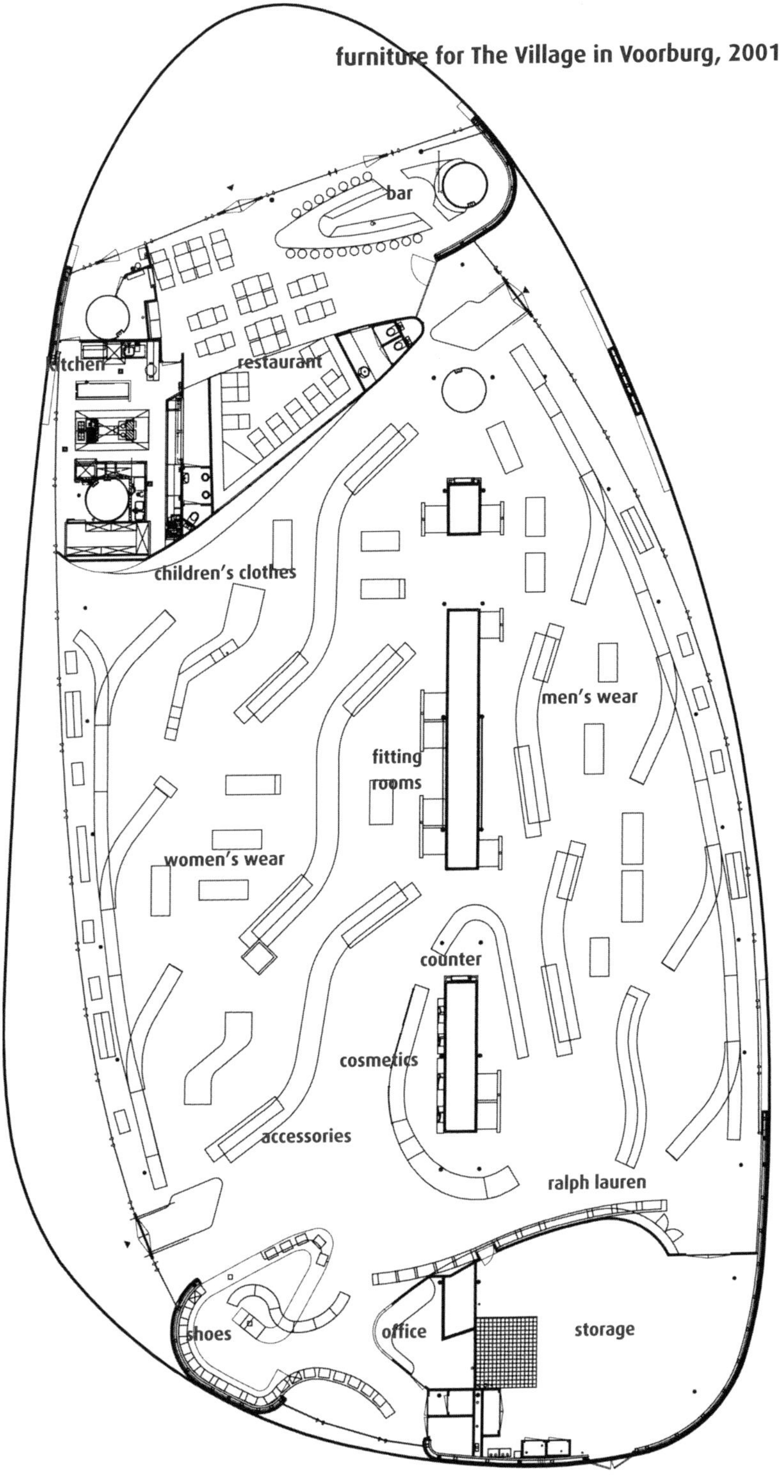

bar

kitchen

restaurant

children's clothes

men's wear

fitting rooms

women's wear

counter

cosmetics

accessories

ralph lauren

shoes

office

storage

White is also the colour of the generic. Just consider the colour RAL 9010 which Richard Meier (to take an example) uses for all his buildings all over the world. It is the colour, and it is that particular colour that denies the existence of colour. Within the process of the standardization of colours and building products, white is the paragon of availability. White is always in stock. White is the whore of the spectrum.

men's wear

furniture for The Village in Voorburg, 2001-2003

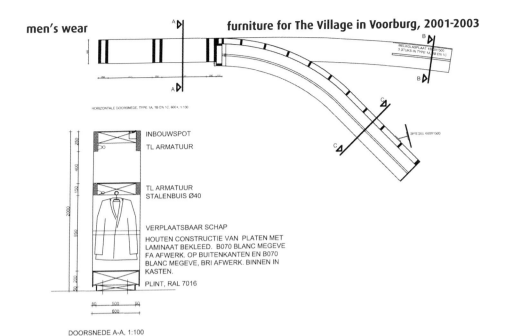

HORIZONTALE DOORSNEDE, TYPE 1A, 1B EN 1C, 600+, 1:100

INBOUWSPOT

TL ARMATUUR

TL ARMATUUR
STALENBUIS Ø40

VERPLAATSBAAR SCHAP

HOUTEN CONSTRUCTIE VAN PLATEN MET
LAMINAAT BEKLEED. B070 BLANC MEGEVE
FA AFWERK. OP BUITENKANTEN EN B070
BLANC MEGEVE, BRI AFWERK. BINNEN IN
KASTEN.

PLINT, RAL 7016

DOORSNEDE A-A, 1:100

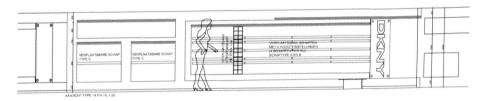

AANZICHT TYPE 1A EN 1B, 1:20

INBOUWSPOT

TL ARMATUUR

STALENBUIS Ø40

MELKGLASPLAAT
1500X1500

INBOUWSPOT

TL ARMATUUR

STALENBUIS Ø40

VERPLAATSBARE
SCHAPPEN MET 5
HOOGTEINSTELLINGEN

STAAL ONDERSTEUNING
MET SPIEGEL BEKLEED

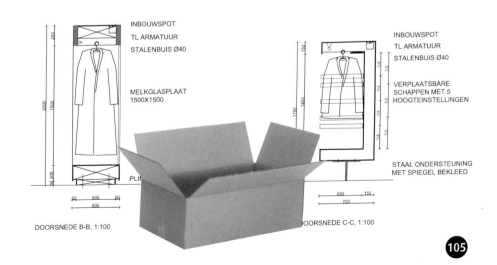

DOORSNEDE B-B, 1:100

DOORSNEDE C-C, 1:100

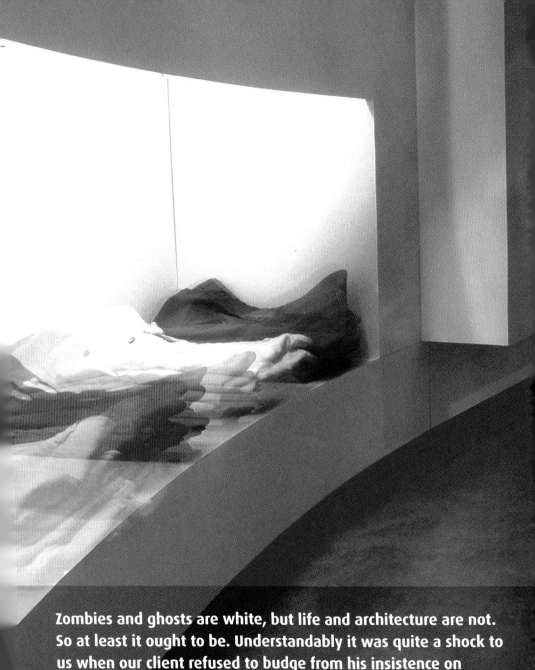

Zombies and ghosts are white, but life and architecture are not. So at least it ought to be. Understandably it was quite a shock to us when our client refused to budge from his insistence on having the whole interior of his shop, including the display furniture, finished in white. A black floor was fine, as were a restaurant with red walls, and benches and a bar also in red. But the shop interior had to be an unmitigated white.

men's wear

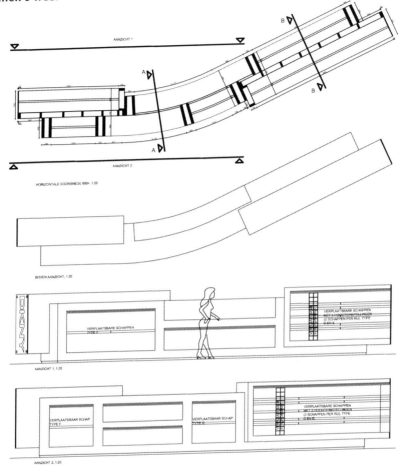

AANZICHT 1

AANZICHT 2

HORIZONTALE DOORSNEDE 800+, 1:20

BOVEN AANZICHT, 1:20

VERPLAATSBARE SCHAPPEN
TYPE I

VERPLAATSBARE SCHAPPEN
MET 5 HOOGTEINSTELLINGEN
(2 SCHAPPEN PER RIJ), TYPE
D EN E

AANZICHT 1, 1:20

VERPLAATSBAAR SCHAP
TYPE F

VERPLAATSBAAR SCHAP
TYPE G

VERPLAATSBARE SCHAPPEN
MET 5 HOOGTEINSTELLINGEN
(2 SCHAPPEN PER RIJ), TYPE
D EN E

AANZICHT 2, 1:20

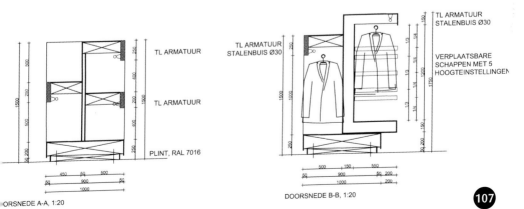

TL ARMATUUR

TL ARMATUUR

PLINT, RAL 7016

DOORSNEDE A-A, 1:20

TL ARMATUUR
STALENBUIS Ø30

TL ARMATUUR
STALENBUIS Ø30

VERPLAATSBARE
SCHAPPEN MET 5
HOOGTEINSTELLINGEN

DOORSNEDE B-B, 1:20

Make a virtue out of necessity, the proverb advises us. OK, then.
Suppose we were to turn the whole idea about white on its
head. Suppose white were the colour of life and all the other
colours stood for death. Suppose that white were the colour of
imperishable things and the rest of the palette stood for that
which is perishable. Suppose that the white interior is the
timeless, immortal carrier for all that is transient

women's wear & accessories　　furniture for The Village in Voorburg, 2001-2003

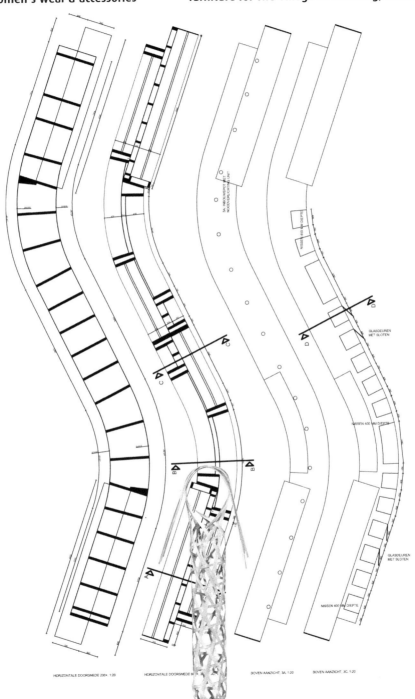

HORIZONTALE DOORSNEDE 200+, 1:20　　HORIZONTALE DOORSNEDE B, 1:20　　BOVEN AANZICHT, 3A, 1:20　　BOVEN AANZICHT, 3C, 1:20

109

A sophistic inversion which holds a measure of validity is that everything displayed in this interior and in these furnishings – the clothes, shoes, cosmetics and accessories – is literally and shamelessly transient. This interior is a carrier of stylistic ephemera and seasonal phantoms; of fashion, in other words. So perhaps it is appropriate that white forms the background to all that colourful flirtation with finality.

women's wear & accessories   furniture for The Village in Voorburg, 2001-2003

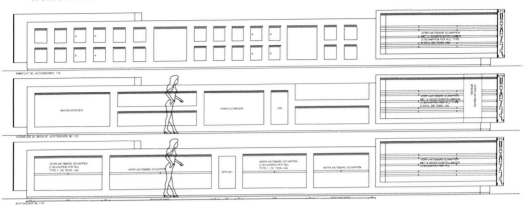

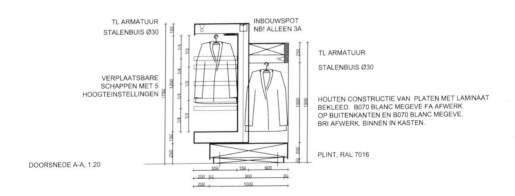

TL ARMATUUR
STALENBUIS Ø30

VERPLAATSBARE
SCHAPPEN MET 5
HOOGTEINSTELLINGEN

INBOUWSPOT
NB! ALLEEN 3A

TL ARMATUUR

STALENBUIS Ø30

HOUTEN CONSTRUCTIE VAN PLATEN MET LAMINAAT
BEKLEED. B070 BLANC MEGEVE FA AFWERK.
OP BUITENKANTEN EN B070 BLANC MEGEVE,
BRI AFWERK. BINNEN IN KASTEN.

PLINT, RAL 7016

DOORSNEDE A-A, 1:20

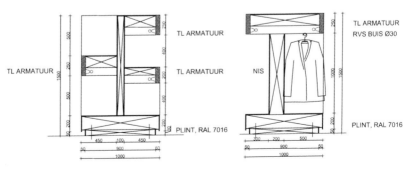

TL ARMATUUR

TL ARMATUUR

TL ARMATUUR

PLINT, RAL 7016

DOORSNEDE B-B, 1:20

TL ARMATUUR
RVS BUIS Ø30

NIS

PLINT, RAL 7016

DOORSNEDE C-C, 1:20

furniture for The Village in Voorburg, built 2003

And perhaps insomnia, formalized in the colour white, can be a quality. Nobody is certain why people and other mammals have to sleep. Bacteria and fish don't sleep. Biologists have posed many theories, but none are universally accepted. Some say that sleep is necessary for dreams, while others hold that you simply need the rest. Perhaps sleep is an unnecessary activity which is kept going by a kind of faith.

women's wear   furniture for The Village in Voorburg, 2001-2003

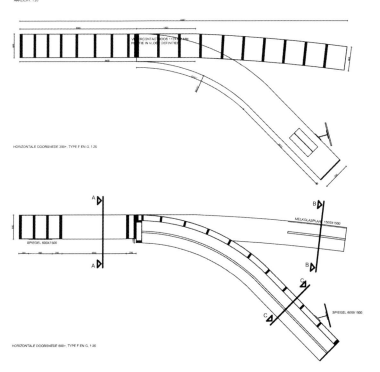

AANZICHT, 1:20

HORIZONTALE DOORSNEDE 200+, TYPE F EN G, 1:20

HORIZONTALE DOORSNEDE 800+, TYPE F EN G, 1:20

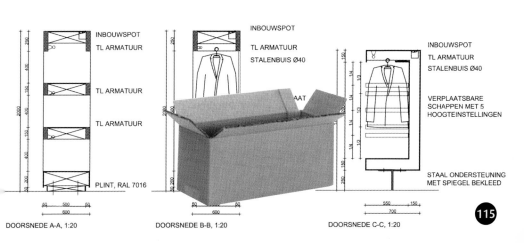

INBOUWSPOT
TL ARMATUUR

TL ARMATUUR

TL ARMATUUR

PLINT, RAL 7016

DOORSNEDE A-A, 1:20

INBOUWSPOT

TL ARMATUUR
STALENBUIS Ø40

DOORSNEDE B-B, 1:20

INBOUWSPOT
TL ARMATUUR
STALENBUIS Ø40

VERPLAATSBARE
SCHAPPEN MET 5
HOOGTEINSTELLINGEN

STAAL ONDERSTEUNING
MET SPIEGEL BEKLEED

DOORSNEDE C-C, 1:20

Or, as the friar declaims in the book The Arabian Nightmare by Robert Irwin, 'Sleep is not a quality but rather the absence of one, that is, wakefulness. No more is dreaming an attribute but rather the denial of one, that is, rationality. (It is as if one were to call a black man "coloured". Which is absurd, for what he actually suffers from is absence of colour, for, as the Blessed Niko tells us, black is not a colour.)'

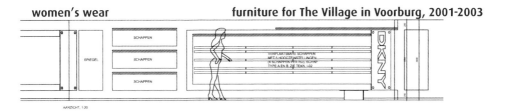

AANZICHT, 1:20

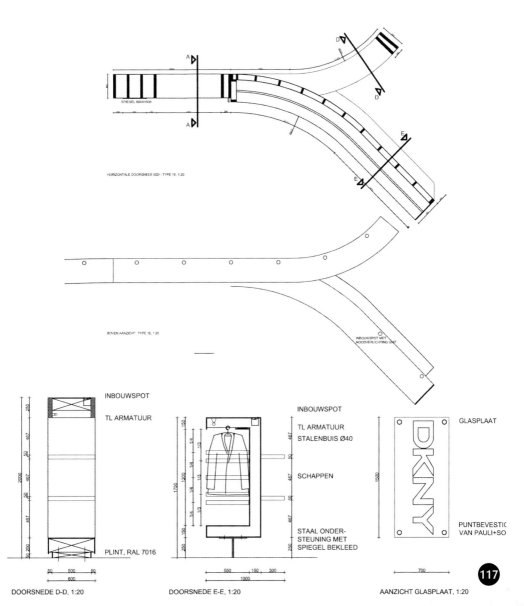

INBOUWSPOT

TL ARMATUUR

PLINT, RAL 7016

DOORSNEDE D-D, 1:20

INBOUWSPOT

TL ARMATUUR
STALENBUIS Ø40

SCHAPPEN

STAAL ONDER-
STEUNING MET
SPIEGEL BEKLEED

DOORSNEDE E-E, 1:20

GLASPLAAT

PUNTBEVESTIG
VAN PAULI+SO

AANZICHT GLASPLAAT, 1:20

This is a rather devastating pronouncement for those people who appreciate the colour black. But, like it or not, the observation carries some weight. Black is really the absence of colour whereas white is the impervious denial of colour. Black greedily absorbs light, whereas white spurns and rejects light. Black is the colour of shadow, white of overexposure. Black is the colour of the wicked witch, white of Snow White.

miscellaneous display furniture   furniture for The Village in Voorburg, 2001-2003

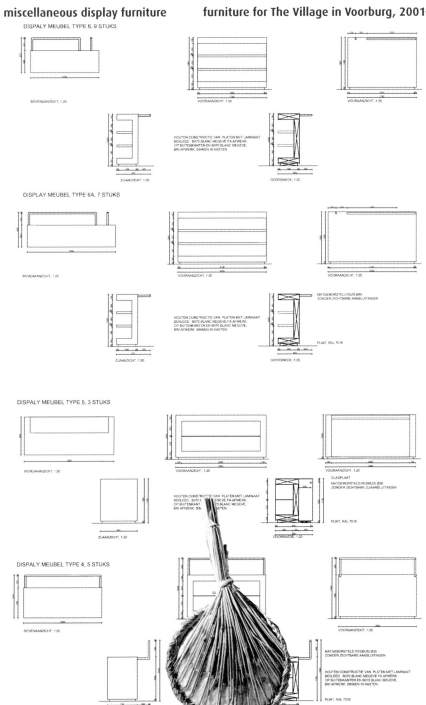

DISPALY MEUBEL TYPE 6, 9 STUKS

BOVENAANZICHT, 1:20

VOORAANZICHT, 1:20

VOORAANZICHT, 1:20

ZIJAANZICHT, 1:20

HOUTEN CONSTRUCTIE VAN PLATEN MET LAMINAAT
BEKLEED. B070 BLANC MEGEVE FA AFWERK
OP BUITENKANTEN EN B070 BLANC MEGEVE.
BRI AFWERK. BINNEN IN KASTEN.

DOORSNEDE, 1:20

DISPLAY MEUBEL TYPE 6A, 7 STUKS

BOVENAANZICHT, 1:20

VOORAANZICHT, 1:20

VOORAANZICHT, 1:20

MATGEBORSTELD BUIS Ø40
ZONDER ZICHTBARE AANSLUITINGEN

ZIJAANZICHT, 1:20

HOUTEN CONSTRUCTIE VAN PLATEN MET LAMINAAT
BEKLEED. B070 BLANC MEGEVE FA AFWERK
OP BUITENKANTEN EN B070 BLANC MEGEVE.
BRI AFWERK. BINNEN IN KASTEN.

PLINT, RAL 7016

DOORSNEDE, 1:20

DISPALY MEUBEL TYPE 5, 3 STUKS

BOVENAANZICHT, 1:20

VOORAANZICHT, 1:20

VOORAANZICHT, 1:20

GLASPLAAT
MATGEBORSTELD RVSBUIS Ø30
ZONDER ZICHTBARE ZIJAANSLUITINGEN

HOUTEN CONSTRUCTIE VAN PLATEN MET LAMINAAT
BEKLEED. B070 BLANC MEGEVE FA AFWERK
OP BUITENKANTEN B070 BLANC MEGEVE.
BRI AFWERK. BINNEN IN KASTEN.

PLINT, RAL 7016

ZIJAANZICHT, 1:20

DOORSNEDE, 1:20

DISPALY MEUBEL TYPE 4, 5 STUKS

BOVENAANZICHT, 1:20

VOORAANZICHT, 1:20

MATGEBORSTELD RVSBUIS Ø30
ZONDER ZICHTBARE AANSLUITINGEN

HOUTEN CONSTRUCTIE VAN PLATEN MET LAMINAAT
BEKLEED. B070 BLANC MEGEVE FA AFWERK
OP BUITENKANTEN EN B070 BLANC MEGEVE.
BRI AFWERK. BINNEN IN KASTEN.

PLINT, RAL 7016

ZIJAANZICHT, 1:20

DOORSNEDE, 1:20

119

So is the colour white the code of this interior, just as the form of an animal is the code of the waste treatment plant? Not really. There is something else that dictated the design of the furnishings. Just look at these photos, in which the clothing and shoes have become silhouettes while the furniture too seems to escape scrutiny because it does not comply with the orthogonal perspective system.

children's clothes   furniture for The Village in Voorburg, 2001-2003

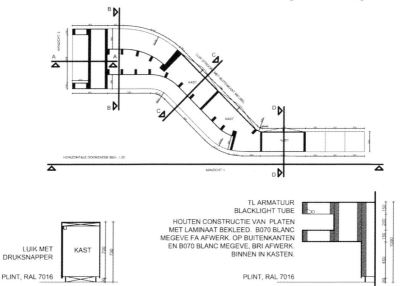

LUIK MET DRUKSNAPPER   KAST

PLINT, RAL 7016

DOORSNEDE D-D, 1:100

TL ARMATUUR BLACKLIGHT TUBE

HOUTEN CONSTRUCTIE VAN PLATEN MET LAMINAAT BEKLEED. B070 BLANC MEGEVE FA AFWERK. OP BUITENKANTEN EN B070 BLANC MEGEVE, BRI AFWERK. BINNEN IN KASTEN.

PLINT, RAL 7016

DOORSNEDE A-A, 1:100

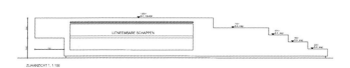

ZIJAANZICHT 1, 1:100

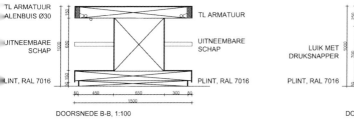

TL ARMATUUR ALENBUIS Ø30

UITNEEMBARE SCHAP

PLINT, RAL 7016

TL ARMATUUR

UITNEEMBARE SCHAP

PLINT, RAL 7016

DOORSNEDE B-B, 1:100

LUIK MET DRUKSNAPPER   KAST

PLINT, RAL 7016

TL ARMATUUR

UITNEEMBARE SCHAP

PLINT, RAL 7016

DOORSNEDE C-C, 1:100

The code is a thread. The furniture as a whole forms a broad, white thread which has been laid down in a meandering course over the black shop floor. A broken white thread which, when seen from above, is hard to reconstruct as a single line. Lagging behind, like a mental after image persisting at eye height, are the capricious kinks of this thread, the idiosyncratic curves of commercialism.

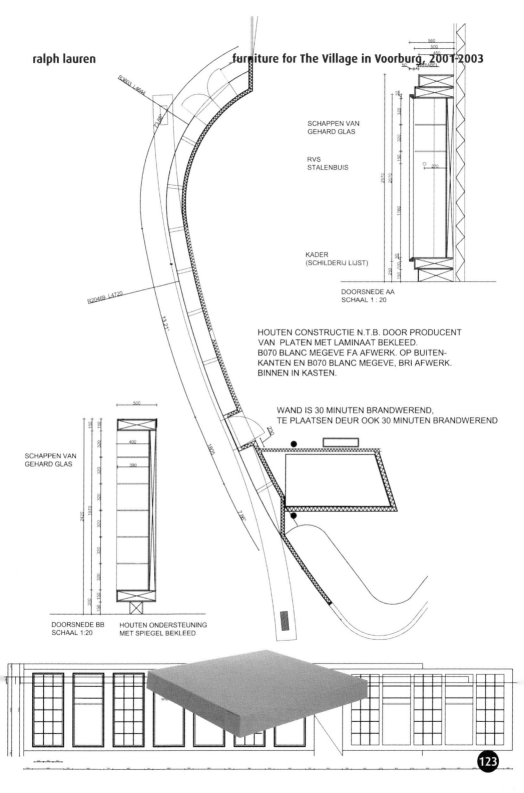

SCHAPPEN VAN
GEHARD GLAS

RVS
STALENBUIS

KADER
(SCHILDERIJ LIJST)

DOORSNEDE AA
SCHAAL 1 : 20

HOUTEN CONSTRUCTIE N.T.B. DOOR PRODUCENT
VAN PLATEN MET LAMINAAT BEKLEED.
B070 BLANC MEGEVE FA AFWERK. OP BUITEN-
KANTEN EN B070 BLANC MEGEVE, BRI AFWERK.
BINNEN IN KASTEN.

WAND IS 30 MINUTEN BRANDWEREND,
TE PLAATSEN DEUR OOK 30 MINUTEN BRANDWEREND

SCHAPPEN VAN
GEHARD GLAS

DOORSNEDE BB   HOUTEN ONDERSTEUNING
SCHAAL 1:20   MET SPIEGEL BEKLEED

furniture for The Village in Voorburg, 2001-2003

How specific can an interior design be when it is intended for seasonal fantasies? Does the classic distinction between the specific and the general-purpose, between the unique and the universal, between haute couture and prêt-à-porter, still exist? Are oppositions of this kind still valid and legible in the present day? Probably they apply now only in the fourth dimension, the dimension of time.

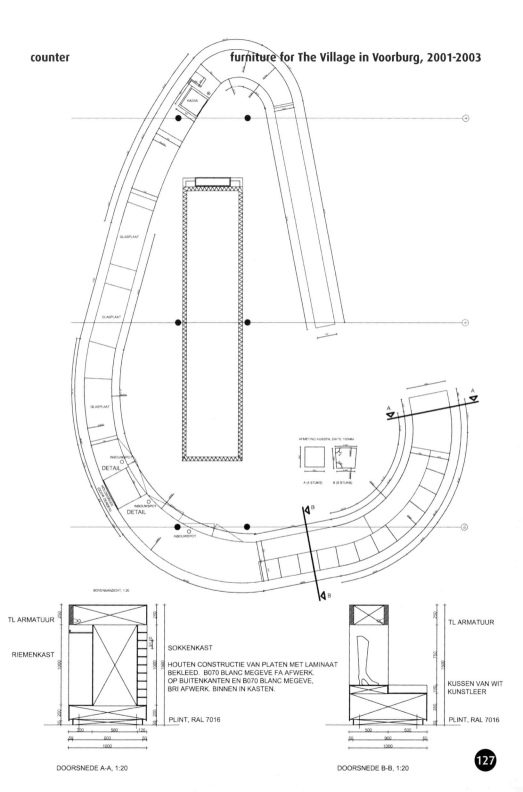

TL ARMATUUR

RIEMENKAST

SOKKENKAST

HOUTEN CONSTRUCTIE VAN PLATEN MET LAMINAAT
BEKLEED. B070 BLANC MEGEVE FA AFWERK.
OP BUITENKANTEN EN B070 BLANC MEGEVE,
BRI AFWERK. BINNEN IN KASTEN.

PLINT, RAL 7016

TL ARMATUUR

KUSSEN VAN WIT
KUNSTLEER

PLINT, RAL 7016

DOORSNEDE A-A, 1:20 DOORSNEDE B-B, 1:20

127

In Flash Art, fashion designer Azzedine Alaïa had the following to say about haute couture: 'The manual procedure is really the essence. Everyone is different and commands a different approach. You build up an understanding with the person you are working with. An atmosphere develops that has nothing to do with the dress. The moments when you are fitting the dress are more important than the big day when the dress is worn.'

cosmetics

furniture for The Village in Voorburg, 2001-2003

BESTAANDE KOLLOM

TOT AAN SPIEGELNAAD

IN HET WERK CONTROLEREN

GLAZEN SCHAPPEN

BESTAANDE KOLLOM

LADE

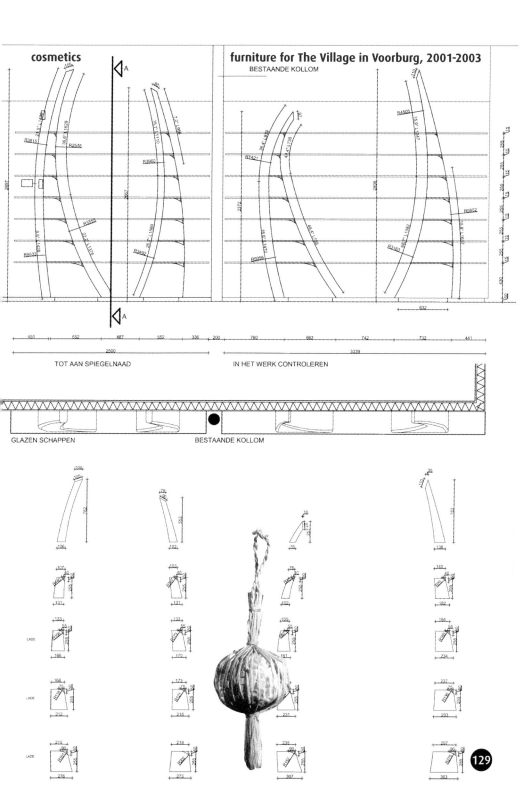

129

Is that the difference between the specific and the general-purpose? That the rehearsals are more important than the premiere, that the discussions about the design sometimes carry more significance than the eventual result? But what criteria do you use to evaluate the outcome? Is the difference between a successful project and an unsuccessful one actually measurable? Or is it merely a cocktail of time and talent?

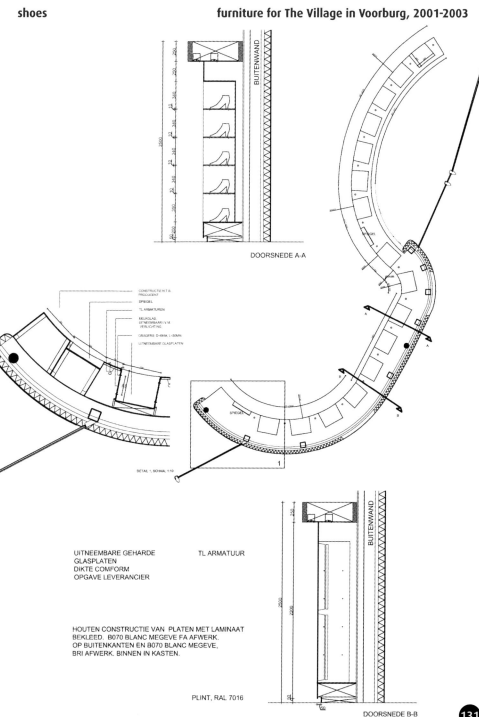

DOORSNEDE A-A

CONSTRUCTIE N.T.B.
PRODUCENT

SPIEGEL

TL ARMATUREN

MELKGLAS
UITNEEMBAAR I.V.M.
VERLICHTING

DRAGERS: D=8MM, L=30MM

UITNEEMBARE GLASPLATEN

DETAIL 1, SCHAAL 1:10

UITNEEMBARE GEHARDE　　　　　TL ARMATUUR
GLASPLATEN
DIKTE COMFORM
OPGAVE LEVERANCIER

HOUTEN CONSTRUCTIE VAN PLATEN MET LAMINAAT
BEKLEED. B070 BLANC MEGEVE FA AFWERK.
OP BUITENKANTEN EN B070 BLANC MEGEVE,
BRI AFWERK. BINNEN IN KASTEN.

PLINT, RAL 7016

DOORSNEDE B-B

One thing is certain: architecture is haute couture. It is always personal, made to measure, unrepeatable and, of course, more expensive than a standardized product. The white, subservient display furnishings are, on consideration, more specific than all those colourful 'artistic' garments. The furniture is timeless in a world of ephemerality. It takes its time to introduce something new into the world, like an obstetrician in a white coat.

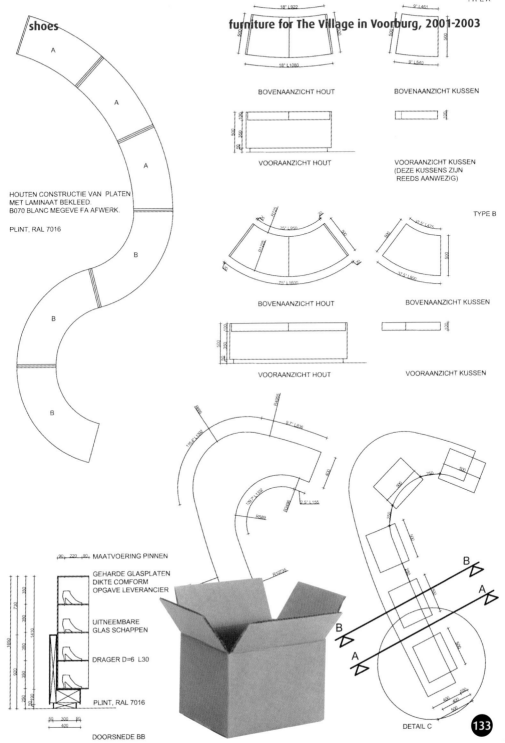

shoes

furniture for The Village in Voorburg, 2001-2003

TYPE A

18° L922

9° L461

18° L1080

9° L540

BOVENAANZICHT HOUT

BOVENAANZICHT KUSSEN

VOORAANZICHT HOUT

VOORAANZICHT KUSSEN
(DEZE KUSSENS ZIJN
REEDS AANWEZIG)

TYPE B

75° L1950

37.5° L475

75° L1600

37.5° L800

BOVENAANZICHT HOUT

BOVENAANZICHT KUSSEN

VOORAANZICHT HOUT

VOORAANZICHT KUSSEN

HOUTEN CONSTRUCTIE VAN PLATEN
MET LAMINAAT BEKLEED.
B070 BLANC MEGEVE FA AFWERK.

PLINT, RAL 7016

A

A

A

B

B

B

MAATVOERING PINNEN

GEHARDE GLASPLATEN
DIKTE COMFORM
OPGAVE LEVERANCIER

UITNEEMBARE
GLAS SCHAPPEN

DRAGER D=6 L30

PLINT, RAL 7016

DOORSNEDE BB

B

B

A

A

DETAIL C

133

Does white stand for insomnia? Does this interior denote a dreamless world? Don't these cabinets dream, then? Of course they do. Just as dogs and other mammals, as people, dream, these furnishings dream of ... well, what do they dream about? They dream of Giorgio Armani, Donna Karen, Ralph Lauren, Calvin Klein and Hugo Boss. Probably they have nightmares about Prada and Mexx.

bar

furniture for The Village in Voorburg, 2001-2003

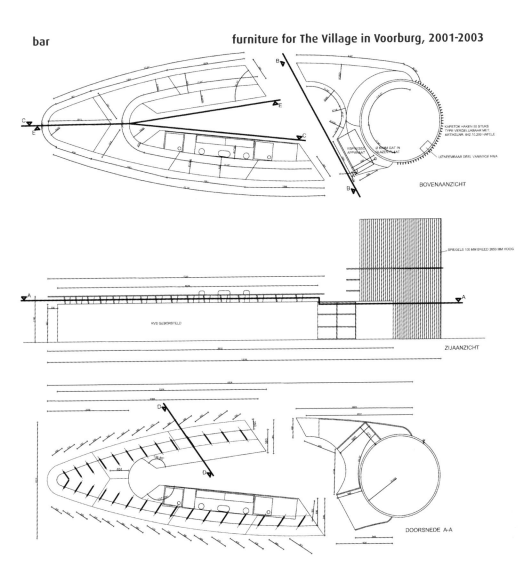

KAPSTOK HAKEN 50 STUKS
TYPE VERGELIJKBAAR MET
ARTIKELNR. 842.10.200 HAFELE

UITNEEMBAAR DEEL VANWEGE HWA

BOVENAANZICHT

ESPRESSO APPARAAT

Ø 60MM GAT IN GLAZEN PLAAT

SPIEGELS 100 MM BREED 2650 MM HOOG

RVS GEBORSTELD

ZIJAANZICHT

DOORSNEDE A-A

BARBLAD:
8/29 GELAAGD GEHARD BLANK FLOATGLAS,
GELAAGD MIDDELS ROOD GEPIGMENTEERDE GIETHARS
EN AAN OMTREK VOORZIEN VAN RVS BAND

TAPZUILEN

SPOELBAK

KOELKAST

KOELLADE

SPOELBAK

LESBENNEST

OPEN BERGRUIMTE

DOORSNEDE C-C

RVS WERKBLAD

HOUTEN ROMP BEKLEEDT
MET GEBORSTELD RVS

KOELKAST

DOORSNEDE D-D

THE BANKRUPTCY OF THE SIGN >

16 September 2003 Dear Tim, yesterday I saw your theatre piece Instructions For Forgetting. It was an intriguing performance, but the meaning of the title eludes me. What exactly is that, an instruction to forget? Do you have to tell stories of yourself and other people in order to forget them? Is that the instruction? Is every narrative an instruction to forget? Is every tale a way of wiping your memory?

05

service building for Wasco Beheer in Rotterdam, 1997-1998

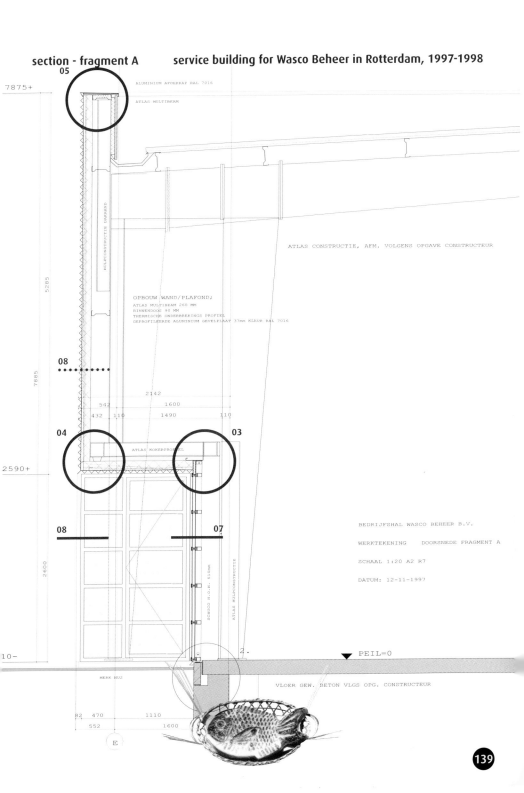

7875+

ALUMINIUM AFDEKKAP RAL 7016

ATLAS MULTIBEAM

HULPCONSTRUCTIE GASRAND

5285

ATLAS CONSTRUCTIE, AFM. VOLGENS OPGAVE CONSTRUCTEUR

OPBOUW WAND/PLAFOND;
ATLAS MULTIBEAM 260 MM
BINNENDOOS 90 MM
THERMISCHE ONDERBREKINGS PROFIEL
GEPROFILEERDE ALUMINIUM GEVELPLAAT 37mm KLEUR RAL 7016

7885

08
● ● ● ● ● ● ● ● ● ● ●

2142

542   1600

432 110   1490   110

04   **03**

ATLAS KOKERPROFIEL

2590+

08   **07**

BEDRIJFSHAL WASCO BEHEER B.V.

WERKTEKENING   DOORSNEDE FRAGMENT A

SCHAAL 1:20 A2 R7

DATUM: 12-11-1997

2600

SCHÜCO H.O.H. 510mm

ATLAS HULPCONSTRUCTIE

10-

2.

▼ PEIL=0

MERK NU2

VLOER GEW. BETON VLGS OPG. CONSTRUCTEUR

82 470   1110

552   1600

E

17 September 2003 I wake up and recall this dream: two friends meet in a large hall. They are rather upset about something. They have received parcels from a mutual friend in the post from various countries – China, Turkey and Sweden. The packages always contained the same thing, a meal, the friend's favourite dish. Pretty bizarre in its own right, but what disturbs them is that their friend has been dead for over a year.

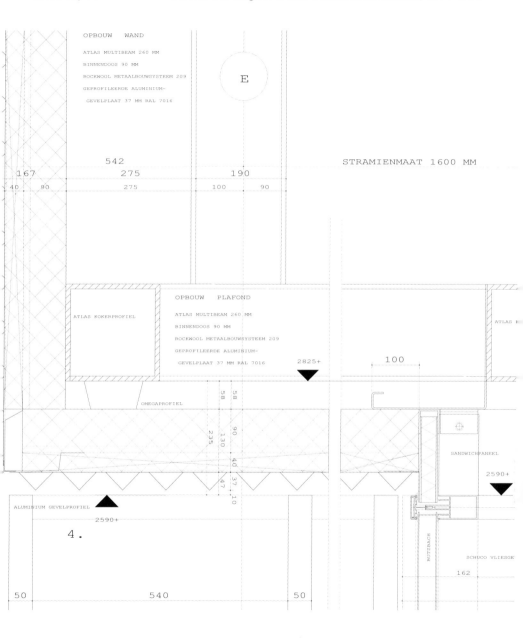

OPBOUW   WAND

ATLAS MULTIBEAM 260 MM

BINNENDOOS 90 MM

ROCKWOOL METAALBOUWSYSTEEM 209

GEPROFILEERDE ALUMINIUM-

GEVELPLAAT 37 MM RAL 7016

E

542
167   275   190
40   90   275   100   90

STRAMIENMAAT 1600 MM

OPBOUW   PLAFOND

ATLAS KOKERPROFIEL

ATLAS MULTIBEAM 260 MM

BINNENDOOS 90 MM

ROCKWOOL METAALBOUWSYSTEEM 209

GEPROFILEERDE ALUMINIUM-

GEVELPLAAT 37 MM RAL 7016

2825+

ATLAS

100

OMEGAPROFIEL

58   58
235   90 130
40
37 47
10

SANDWICHPANEEL

2590+

ALUMINIUM GEVELPROFIEL

2590+

4.

BUTZBACH

SCHÜCO VLIESGE

162

50   540   50

18 September 2003 Dear Tim, was this dream an instruction to forget? Is this story a way of erasing certain incidents which are about to happen, or is it made up of experiences from the past? Or is there something else? Do I have to tell you this story in order to forget it? Is it a matter of symbolic exchange – say, I give you a story and you give me a chance to erase certain passages from my past present and future?

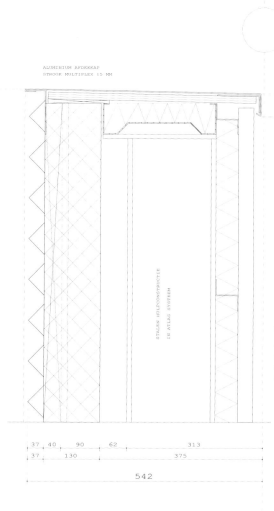

ALUMINIUM AFDEKKAP
STROOK MULTIPLEX 15 MM

DAKRANDCONSTRUCTIE

VOLGENS OPGAVE ATLAS

STALEN HULPCONSTRUCTIE
IN ATLAS SYSTEEM

OPBOUW   WAND

ATLAS MULTIBEAM 260 MM

BINNENDOOS 90 MM

ROCKWOOL METAALBOUWSYSTEEM 209

GEPROFILEERDE ALUMINIUM-
GEVELPLAAT 37 MM RAL 7016

| 37 | 40 | 90 | 62 | 313 |
| 37 | 130 | | | 375 |

542

19 September 2003 Yesterday I dined at a friend's house. Her Taiwanese student prepared a delicious meal. As a token of gratitude, I gave him a book. Then he gave me an orange-coloured amulet which his mother had made and was meant to bring good luck. Cycling home with that thing in my hand, I was struck by a car. For a while I lay unconscious on the ground. They thought I was dead.

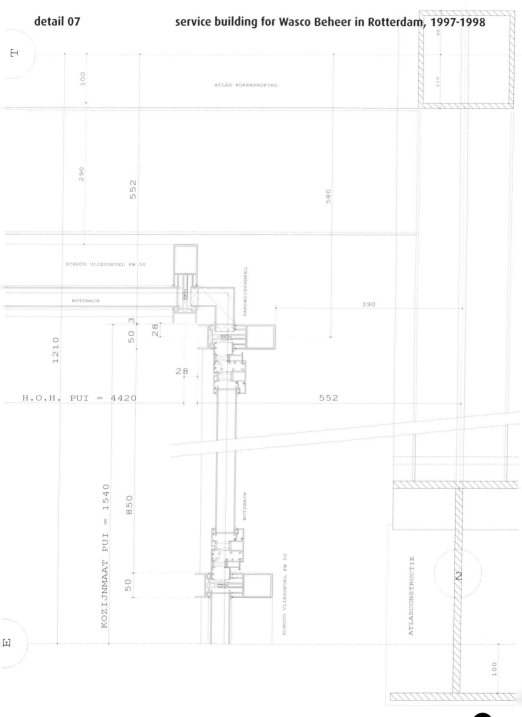

ATLAS KOKERPROFIEL

SCHUCO VLIESGEVEL FW 50

BUTZBACH

SANDWICHPANEEL

H.O.H. PUI = 4420

BUTZBACH

SCHUCO VLIESGEVEL FW 50

ATLASCONSTRUCTIE

KOZIJNMAAT PUI = 1540

20 September 2003 Dear Tim, the next morning I showed off my injuries to my nine-year old son Axel, and then showed him the orange amulet which I had hung above the kitchen door. I asked him: what do you think, does it bring good luck or bad luck? He said, let's leave it up there for a week and see what happens. If it brings bad luck, we can give it to the team I'm playing football against next Saturday.

service building for Wasco Beheer in Rotterdam, 1997-1998

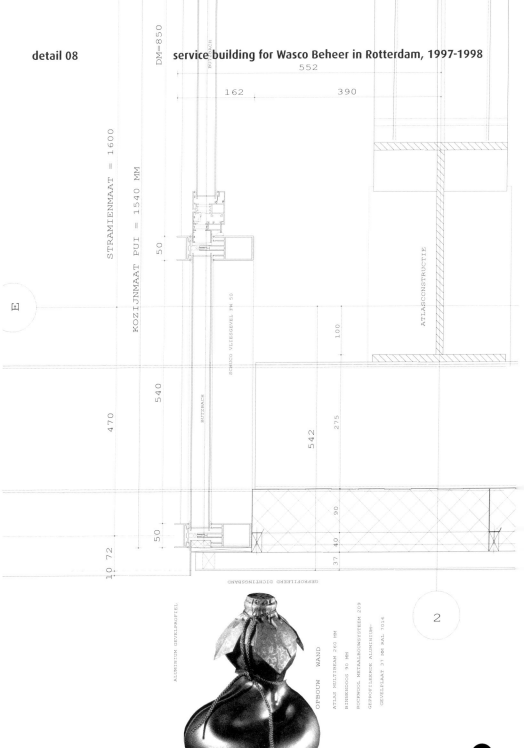

21 September 2003 A clear, instructive, indeed clinical answer. But still unsolved is the question of the meaning of the two incidents – the dream and the accident. Is there a covert message, a code, in their coincidence? Is this an instance of an instruction? After all, things don't happen without reason, do they? The succession of events itself tells a story that you ought to listen to.

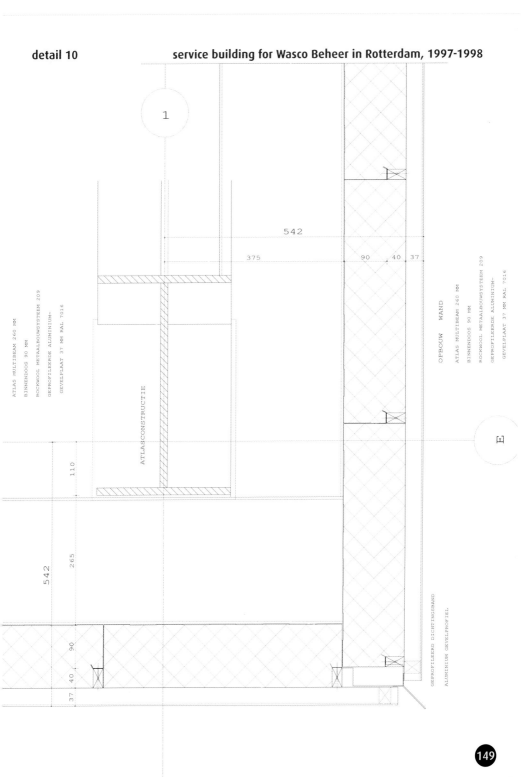

service building for Wasco Beheer in Rotterdam, 1997-1998

22 September 2003 Dear Tim, suddenly I remember the text: the dismissal of the childhood dream, which I wrote in 1988. It is about the power of childhood dreams and the way they can take material shape all too quickly often with disastrous consequences. There is only one remedy – to tell children a bedtime story which pre-empts and eradicates 'their fantasies, perversities and effronteries'.

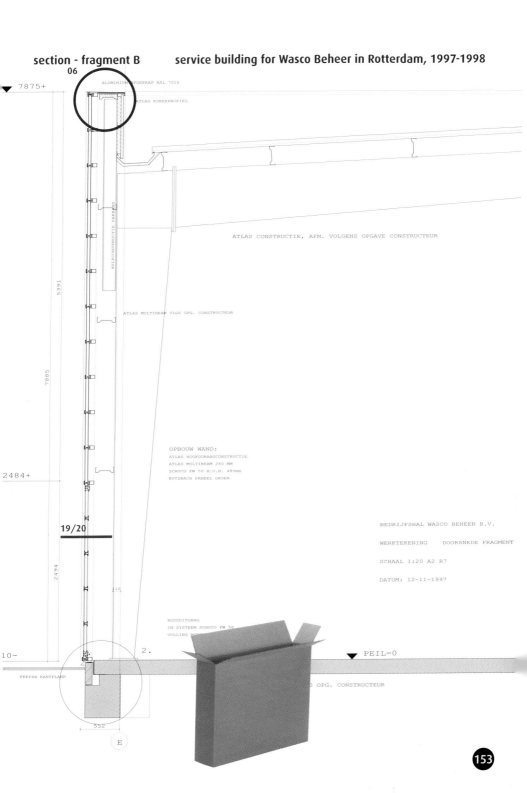

service building for Wasco Beheer in Rotterdam, 1997-1998

7875+

ALUMINIUM AFDEKKAP RAL 7016

ATLAS KOKERPROFIEL

5391

HULPCONSTRUCTIE CAMPANDI

ATLAS CONSTRUCTIE, AFM. VOLGENS OPGAVE CONSTRUCTEUR

ATLAS MULTIBEAM VLGS OPG. CONSTRUCTEUR

7885

OPBOUW WAND:
ATLAS HOOFDDRAAGCONSTRUCTIE
ATLAS MULTIBEAM 260 MM
SCHUCO FW 50 H.O.H. 489mm
BUTZBACH PANEEL GROEN

2484+

19/20

BEDRIJFSHAL WASCO BEHEER B.V.

WERKTEKENING   DOORSNEDE FRAGMENT

SCHAAL 1:20 A2 R7

DATUM: 12-11-1997

2494

110

NOODUITGANG
IN SYSTEEM SCHUCO FW 50
VULLING RUIT

10-

2.

PEIL=0

PREFAB KANTPLANK

G OPG. CONSTRUCTEUR

552

E

23 September 2003 It's not only that a series of happenings can make up a story, but conversely stories and dreams are capable of eliciting and begetting events. The same applies even to thoughts. You have to be careful what you think. Before you know it, a thought has become reality. Before you realize it is happening, your wish comes true and you are answerable for the consequences.

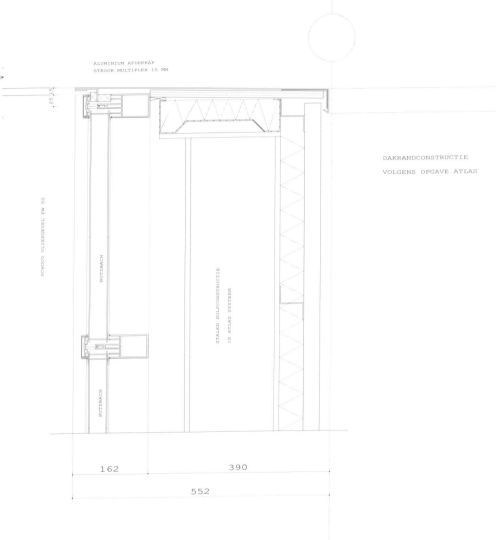

ALUMINIUM AFDEKKAP
STROOK MULTIPLEX 15 MM

DAKRANDCONSTRUCTIE

VOLGENS OPGAVE ATLAS

SCHUCO VLIESGEVEL FW 50

BUTZBACH

BUTZBACH

STALEN HULPCONSTRUCTIE
IN ATLAS SYSTEEM

162   390

552

24 September 2003 Dear Tim, one part of your performance Instructions For Forgetting stays in my mind. You showed a short film in which your little son told the story of the sinking of the Titanic. Then you talked about narrative efficiency. In contrast to James Cameron's bombastic, expensive production, your son told the story in just one minute, and with just as much dramatic impact.

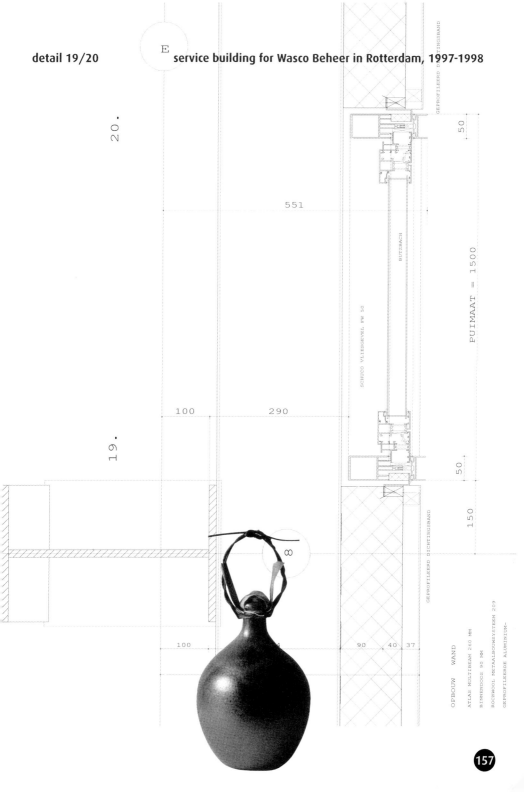

detail 19/20

E service building for Wasco Beheer in Rotterdam, 1997-1998

20.

19.

8

551

100 290

100 90 40 37

GEPROFILEERD DICHTINGSBAND

SCHUCO VLIESGEVEL FW 50

BUTZBACH

50

PUIMAAT = 1500

50

150

GEPROFILEERD DICHTINGSBAND

OPBOUW WAND
ATLAS MULTIBEAM 260 MM
BINNENDOOS 90 MM
ROCKWOOL METAALBOUWSYSTEEM 209
GEPROFILEERDE ALUMINIUM-

25 September 2003 It reminds me of a black building I built in Rotterdam six years ago. The urban context had the same ferocious impact as your son's account of the Titanic. However, there were opportunities present in the architectural conditions. The aesthetic committee of the planning department had rejected the first design by the previous architect. Fired by ideas of narrative efficiency I completed the design in one hour.

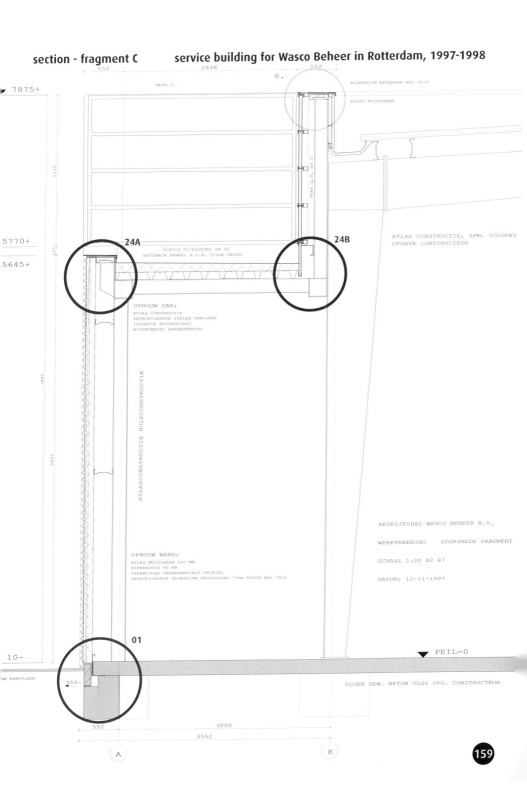

7875+

552   2448   552

6.

MERK T.

ALUMINIUM AFDEKKAP RAL 7016

ATLAS MULTIBEAM

2105

MERK Q, R, EN S

5770+

5645+

24A

24B

ATLAS CONSTRUCTIE, AFM. VOLGENS
OPGAVE CONSTRUCTEUR

SCHUCO VLIESGEVEL FW 50
BUTZBACH PANEEL H.O.H. 510mm GROEN

OPBOUW DAK;
ATLAS CONSTRUCTIE
GEPROFILEERDE STALEN DAKPLAAT
ISOLATIE AFSCHOTLAAG
BITUMINEUZE DAKBEDEKKING;

ATLASCONSTRUCTIE HULPCONSTRUCTIE

OPBOUW WAND;
ATLAS MULTIBEAM 260 MM
BINNENDOOS 90 MM
THERMISCHE ONDERBREKINGS PROFIEL
GEPROFILEERDE ALUMINIUM GEVELPLAAT 37mm KLEUR RAL 7016

BEDRIJFSHAL WASCO BEHEER B.V.

WERKTEKENING   DOORSNEDE FRAGMENT

SCHAAL 1:20 A2 R7

DATUM: 12-11-1997

01

10-

AB KANTPLANK

350-

PEIL=0

VLOER GEW. BETON VLGS OPG. CONSTRUCTEUR

552   3000

3552

A   K

159

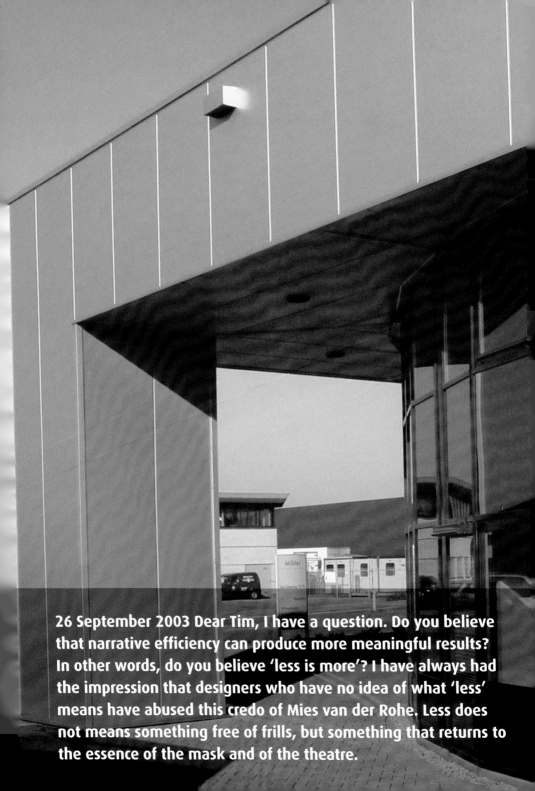

26 September 2003 Dear Tim, I have a question. Do you believe that narrative efficiency can produce more meaningful results? In other words, do you believe 'less is more'? I have always had the impression that designers who have no idea of what 'less' means have abused this credo of Mies van der Rohe. Less does not means something free of frills, but something that returns to the essence of the mask and of the theatre.

detail 01

service building for Wasco Beheer in Rotterdam, 1997-1998

OPBOUW   WAND

ATLAS MULTIBEAM 260 MM

BINNENDOOS 90 MM

ROCKWOOL METAALBOUWSYSTEEM 209

GEPROFILEERDE ALUMINIUM-

GEVELPLAAT 37 MM RAL 7016

37 40   90   375

10   542

ATLASCONSTRUCTIE

PEIL=0

20-

20

200

GEWAPEND BETONVLOER
VLOERBEL. 2500 KG/M2

RBESTRATING 100-

BETONNEN KANTPLANK
100 X 300 MM

350-

200

10   VERBREDING FUNDERING

410

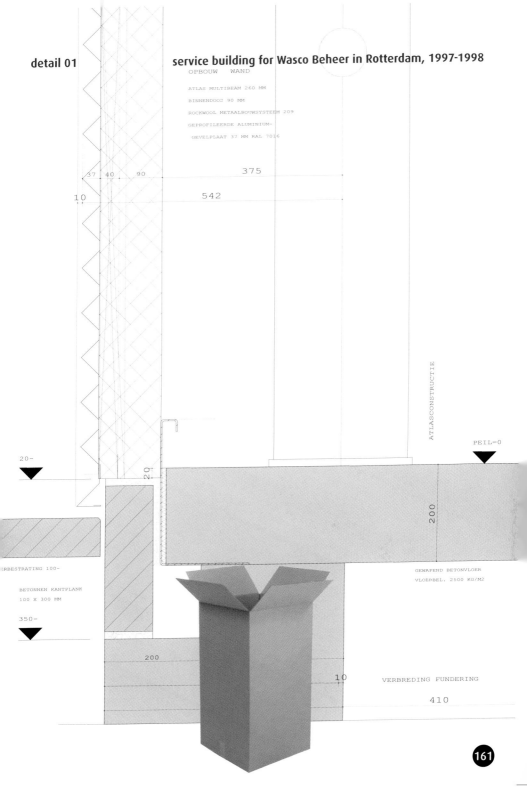

27 September 2003 There is not all that much point in trying to give form to the content. You have to try to give content to the form – not to seek the essence or the 'identity' of the functional programme, but pure semblance and the faceless mask, all this done with the least possible use of resources or straining after effect. The result, in this case, is a cool, black metal box with insets of translucent green fibreglass.

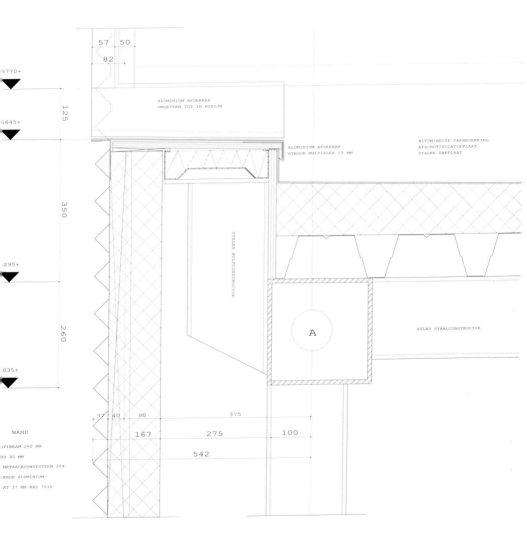

28 September 2003 Dear Tim, did you ever see the film Darkman from 1990? The lead character is a scientist who literally loses his face and desperately tries to find it again. In his secret laboratory, he succeeds in creating a synthetic skin, but it peels off and his mask becomes useless in less than 2 hours - to be exact, in 99 minutes. Isn't this an allegory for the desperate quest for identity?

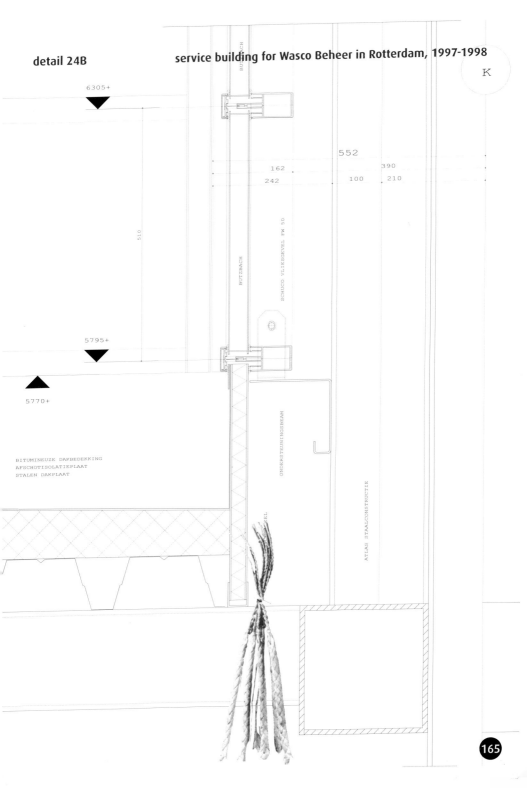

6305+

552

162

242

390

100 210

510

BUTZBACH

SCHUCO VLIESGEVEL FW 50

5795+

5770+

BITUMINEUZE DAKBEDEKKING
AFSCHOTISOLATIEPLAAT
STALEN DAKPLAAT

ONDERSTEUNINGSBEAM

ATLAS STAALCONSTRUCTIE

service building for Waren Beheer in Rotterdam_1992–1948

29 September 2003 The hopelessness of this quest is evident in the photos above. Commercial buildings like these employ all kinds of architectural tricks to put on a show of identity, to stand out from the rest. It is not a real face, but it will last for that 99 minutes. The black WASCO headquarters building takes exactly the opposite approach. It uses a strategy of erasure, of vanishing behind a mask.

7875+

ALUMINIUM AFDEKKAP RAL 7016

25B

5944+

ATLAS CONSTRUCTIE, AFM. VOLGENS

OPGAVE CONSTRUCTEUR

OPBOUW WAND;

ATLAS MULTIBEAM 260 MM

BINNENDOOS 90 MM

THERMISCHE ONDERBREKINGS PROFIEL

GEPROFILEERDE ALUMINIUM GEVELPLAAT 37mm

37mm KLEUR RAL 7016

OPSLAG

25A

4000+

25.

POSTKAMPLAFOND

32.

16

KANTOOR   BEDRIJFSHAL WASCO BEHEER B.V.

WERKTEKENING   DOORSNEDE FRAGMENT E1

SCHAAL 1:20 A2 R7

DATUM: 12-11-1997

AANRIJBEVEILIGING

23

PEIL=0

SCHUCCO FW 50 H.O.H. 492mm

BUTIMACH PAKSEL GROEN

RIB-CASSETTEVLOER 320mm RC 2,5

VLGS OPG. CONSTRUCTEUR

6955(TOT AS)

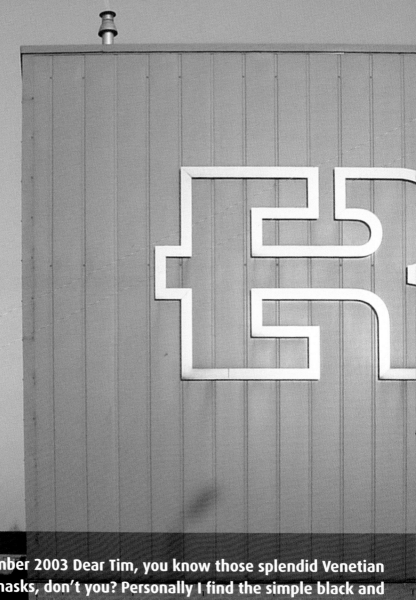

30 September 2003 Dear Tim, you know those splendid Venetian carnival masks, don't you? Personally I find the simple black and white masks the most beautiful ones. When I see someone wearing a Venetian carnival mask, I never get the feeling that the wearer is wearing it to hide his or her identity. They wear it in order to assume a different identity, to have the chance of vanishing and reappearing as someone else.

detail 16

service building for Wasco Beheer in Rotterdam, 1997-1998

N

HULPCONSTRUCTIE

BEAM 260 MM

390

552

580

416

FRAME T.B.V HEFDEUR

FRAME T.B.V HEFDEUR

VLIESGEVEL FW 50

164

SANDWICHPANEEL

28

STRAMIENMAAT = 5744

552

28

H. PUI = 4420

4

BUTZBACH HEFDEUR TYPE HT/40

ALUMINIUM GEZET PROFIEL
2 MM ISOLATIE
SCHÜCO VLIESGEVEL FW 50

H.O.H. PUI = 5000

245

164

BEVESTIGING VLIESGEVEL

BUTZBACH

164

171

1 October 2003 Perhaps that is the essence of the WASCO Building. It wasn't built to conceal something but to create an opportunity for something to vanish. The black facade is a mask behind which there is no face, no identity, waiting to be discovered. I guess that is also the essence of the 'less is more' credo. The art is to reduce everything to a mask, to an inscrutable, deeply ingrained surface.

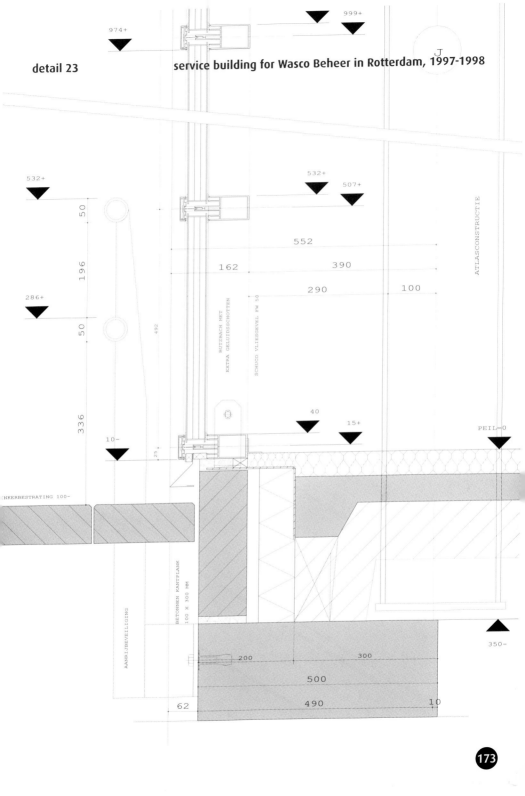

detail 23

service building for Wasco Beheer in Rotterdam, 1997-1998

J

974+

999+

532+

532+

507+

ATLASCONSTRUCTIE

50

552

196

162

390

290

100

286+

50

492

BUTZBACH MET
EXTRA GELUIDSSCHOTTEN

SCHÜCO VLIESGEVEL FW 50

336

40

15+

10-

25+

PEIL=0

NKERBESTRATING 100-

BETONNEN KANTPLANK
100 x 300 MM

350-

AANRIJBEVEILIGING

200

300

500

62

490

10

173

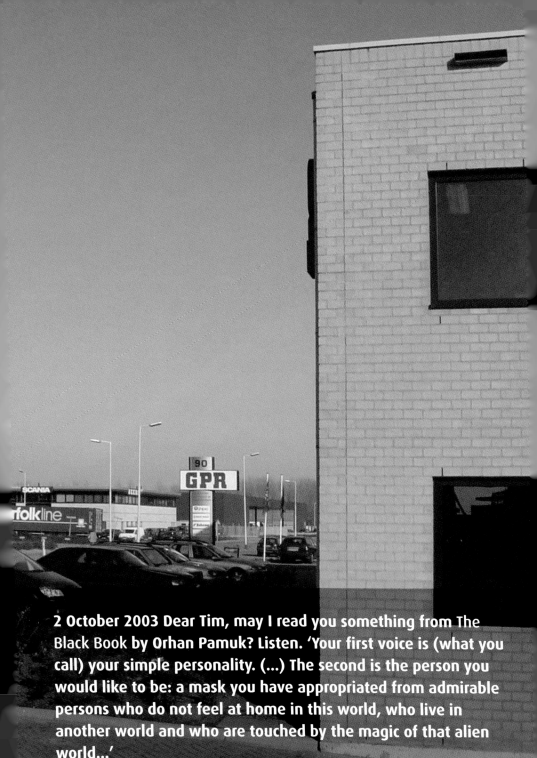

2 October 2003 Dear Tim, may I read you something from The Black Book by Orhan Pamuk? Listen. 'Your first voice is (what you call) your simple personality. (...) The second is the person you would like to be: a mask you have appropriated from admirable persons who do not feel at home in this world, who live in another world and who are touched by the magic of that alien world...'

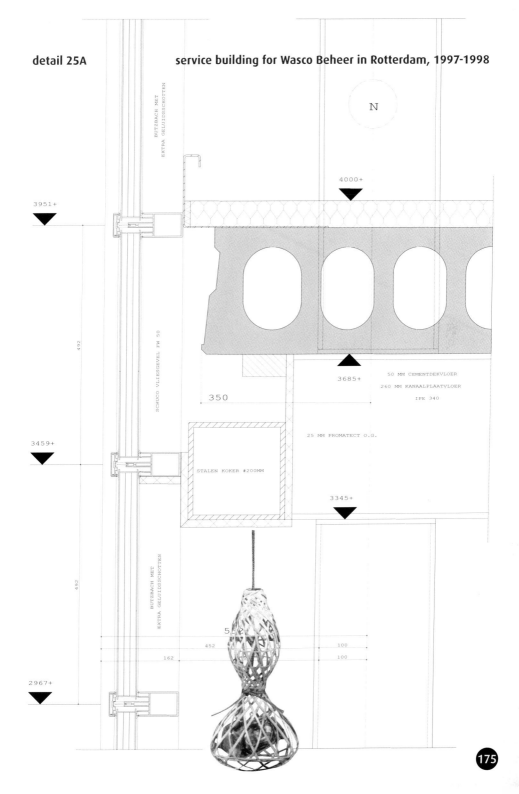

N

3951+

4000+

3685+

3459+

350

3345+

50 MM CEMENTDEKVLOER

260 MM KANAALPLAATVLOER

IPE 340

25 MM PROMATECT O.G.

STALEN KOKER #200MM

BUTZBACH MET EXTRA GELUIDSSCHOTTEN

SCHÜCO VLIESGEVEL FW 50

BUTZBACH MET EXTRA GELUIDSSCHOTTEN

492

492

5.2

452

162

100

100

2967+

175

3 October 2003 'And the third brings you, and me too of course, to worlds where those other two, which you call the "objective style" and the "subjective style", cannot take you: the dark personality, the black style. What you write during those nights when you feel so unhappy that you draw no comfort from imitation or masks is something I know better than you. But what you do about it you know better than I do, my brother.'

detail 25B

service building for Wasco Beheer in Rotterdam, 1997-1998

N

OPBOUW WAND

ATLAS MULTIBEAM 260 MM

BINNENDOOS 90 MM

ROCKWOOL METAALBOUWSYSTEEM 209

GEPROFILEERDE ALUMINIUM-
 GEVELPLAAT 37 MM RAL 7016

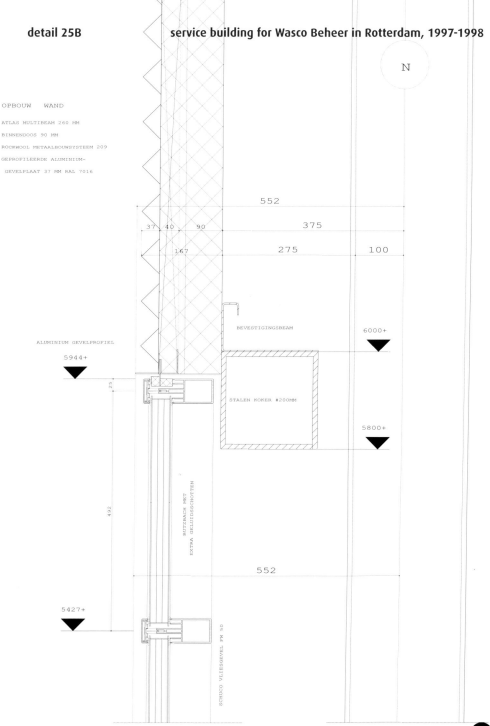

552

37 40   90

375

167

275

100

BEVESTIGINGSBEAM

6000+

ALUMINIUM GEVELPROFIEL

5944+

25

STALEN KOKER #200MM

5800+

492

BUTZBACH MET
EXTRA GELUIDSSCHOTTEN

552

5427+

SCHÜCO VLIESGEVEL FW 50

service building for Waco Beheer in Rotterdam, 1997-1998

4 October 2003 Dear Tim, yesterday I watched the film Darkness
(2002). A family with a little boy moved into a house that has
stood empty for forty years. The house has something spooky
about it. Six children were once viciously murdered here, and a
seventh escaped. Now he has come back, that child, the
concluding sacrifice for which the house has been waiting all
those years. Suddenly, permanent darkness falls.

section - fragment E2   service building for Wasco Beheer in Rotterdam, 1997-1998

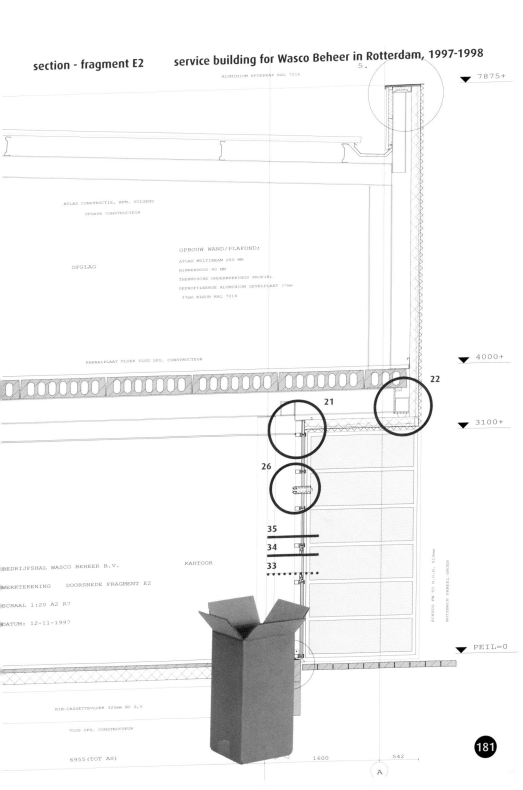

5.

ALUMINIUM AFDEKKAP RAL 7016

▼ 7875+

ATLAS CONSTRUCTIE, AFM. VOLGENS
OPGAVE CONSTRUCTEUR

OPBOUW WAND/PLAFOND;
ATLAS MULTIBEAM 260 MM
BINNENDOOS 90 MM
THERMISCHE ONDERBREKINGS PROFIEL
GEPROFILEERDE ALUMINIUM GEVELPLAAT 37mm
37mm KLEUR RAL 7016

OPSLAG

KANAALPLAAT VLOER VLGS OPG. CONSTRUCTEUR

▼ 4000+

22

21

▼ 3100+

26

35

34

33

BEDRIJFSHAL WASCO BEHEER B.V.   KANTOOR

WERKTEKENING   DOORSNEDE FRAGMENT E2

SCHAAL 1:20 A2 R7

DATUM: 12-11-1997

SCHUCO FW 50 H.O.H. 510mm

BUTZBACH PANEEL GROEN

▼ PEIL=0

RIB-CASSETTEVLOER 320mm RC 2,5

VLGS OPG. CONSTRUCTEUR

181

6955(TOT AS)   1600   542

A

5 October 2003 I have always wondered if it is possible to design a house or other building that places itself open to invasion by inhuman forces? Usually only old houses are capable of that, and then only in films. They are houses with a sinister past; frustrated houses. A new house cannot be haunted. Or, if it is, it must have been built sacrilegiously on an ancient holy place or a cemetery.

service building for Wasco Beheer in Rotterdam, 1997-1998

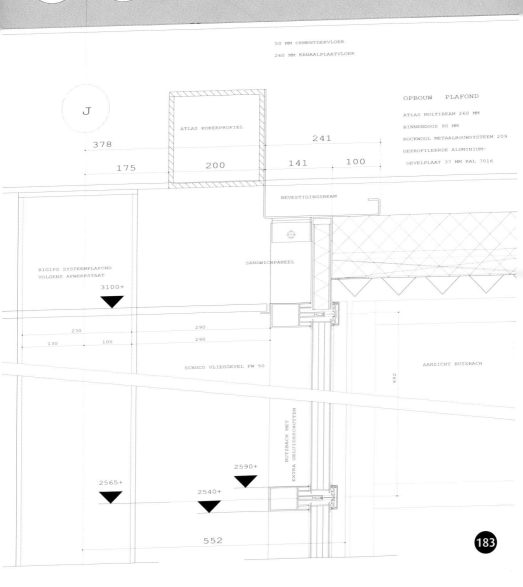

50 MM CEMENTDEKVLOER

260 MM KANAALPLAATVLOER

J

ATLAS KOKERPROFIEL

378

175   200

241

141   100

OPBOUW   PLAFOND

ATLAS MULTIBEAM 260 MM

BINNENDOOS 90 MM

ROCKWOOL METAALBOUWSYSTEEM 209

GEPROFILEERDE ALUMINIUM-

GEVELPLAAT 37 MM RAL 7016

BEVESTIGINGSBEAM

RIGIPS SYSTEEMPLAFOND
VOLGENS AFWERKSTAAT

3100+

SANDWICHPANEEL

230   290

130   100   290

SCHUCO VLIESGEVEL FW 50

AANZICHT BUTZBACH

492

BUTZBACH MET
EXTRA GELUIDSSCHOTTEN

2590+

2565+

2540+

552

6 October 2003 Dear Tim, how many cupboards do you have in your house? Don't you agree we should give new houses much more by way of boxrooms, attics and cellars, so that the sublunary realm may be stored there? I once read that Le Corbusier made all such secondary spaces impossible. Haunted rooms have been taboo ever since plan libre. But I regard the WASCO Building as one huge cupboard.

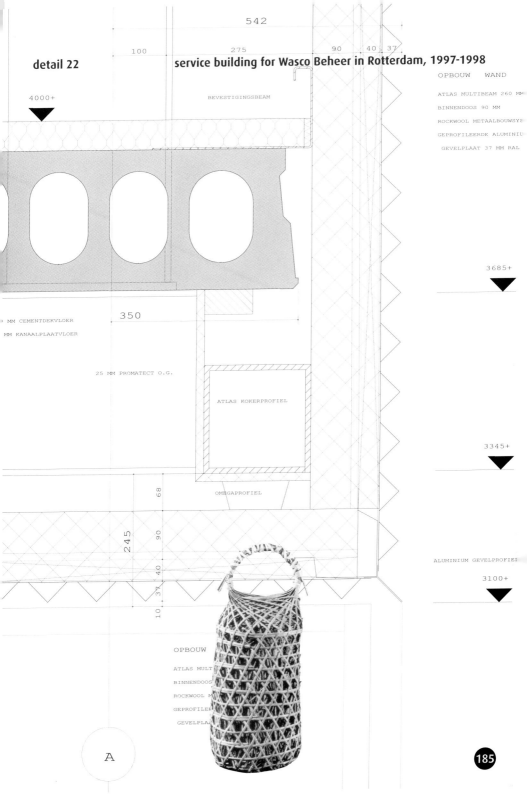

detail 22

service building for Wasco Beheer in Rotterdam, 1997-1998

542

100   275   90   40   37

OPBOUW   WAND

ATLAS MULTIBEAM 260 MM
BINNENDOOS 90 MM
ROCKWOOL METAALBOUWSYS
GEPROFILEERDE ALUMINIU
GEVELPLAAT 37 MM RAL

4000+

BEVESTIGINGSBEAM

3685+

MM CEMENTDEKVLOER

MM KANAALPLAATVLOER

350

25 MM PROMATECT O.G.

ATLAS KOKERPROFIEL

3345+

68

245   90

OMEGAPROFIEL

40

ALUMINIUM GEVELPROFIEL

37

3100+

10

OPBOUW

ATLAS MULT
BINNENDOOS
ROCKWOOL N
GEPROFILEF
GEVELPLA

A

185

7 October 2003 The human spirit also has its cupboards. They take the form of dreams and hallucinations. Usually I am inclined to clear cupboards out, but maybe it is better to leave the clutter for what it is. It is also better not to analyse dreams too much. It doesn't get you anywhere. The real problem is if you are schizophrenic. That means everything has turned into a cupboard. The space has vanished. Pure pigeonhole mentality.

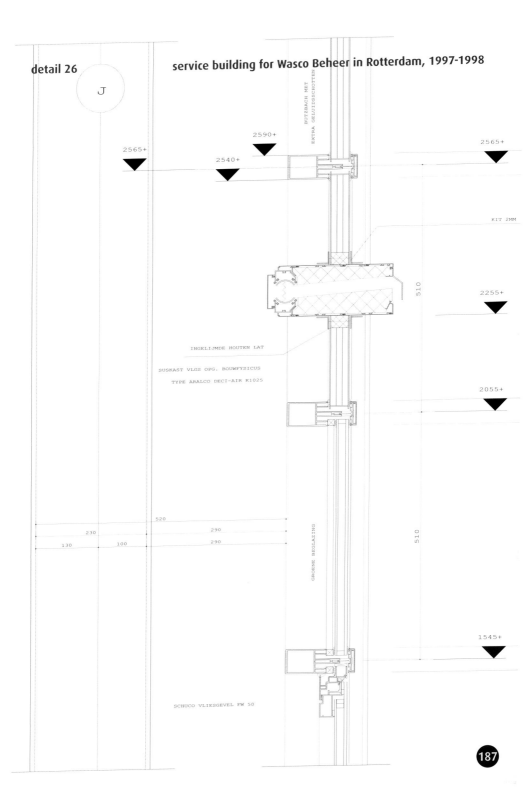

J

2590+

2540+

2565+

2565+

KIT 2MM

BUTZBACH MET
EXTRA GELUIDSSCHOTTEN

510

2255+

INGELIJMDE HOUTEN LAT

SUSKAST VLGS OPG. BOUWFYSICUS

TYPE ARALCO DECI-AIR K1025

2055+

520

230

290

130   100   290

510

GROENE BEGLAZING

1545+

SCHUCO VLIESGEVEL FW 50

187

8 October 2003 Dear Tim, just saw the film Identity. A murderer with a multiple personality is induced under hypnosis to give rein to his ten different identities in a remote motel. The ten personalities are supposed to kill one another one by one until his true, good personality triumphs and proves his innocence. Unfortunately, his nice, good Id is polished off by one of the baddies, an unscrupulous, spiteful child. Always that child.

RAMIENMAAT =5000

detail 33

415 137

service building for Wasco Beheer in Rotterdam, 1997-1998

SANDWICHPANEEL

137 112 112

25

162

BUTZBACH MET
EXTRA GELUIDSSCHOTTEN

552

390

SCHUCO VLIESGEVEL FW 50

415

BUTZBACH MET
EXTRA GELUIDSSCHOTTEN

H.O.H. PUI = 2950

PUIMAAT = 3000

J

552

390 162

116

1

GEPROFILEERD DICHTINGSBAND

542

275 90 40 37

9 October 2003 'The idea of the whole of nature as totally knowable has also suffered a terrible blow with the discovery of dark matter. It now turns out that ninety to ninety-nine per cent of matter in the Universe is utterly unknown to us. It's as if physics has discovered the cosmic unconscious. Dark matter determines the structure and fate of the Universe, and yet we haven't a clue about what it is.' (Rupert Sheldrake)

service building for Wasco Beheer in Rotterdam, 1997-1998

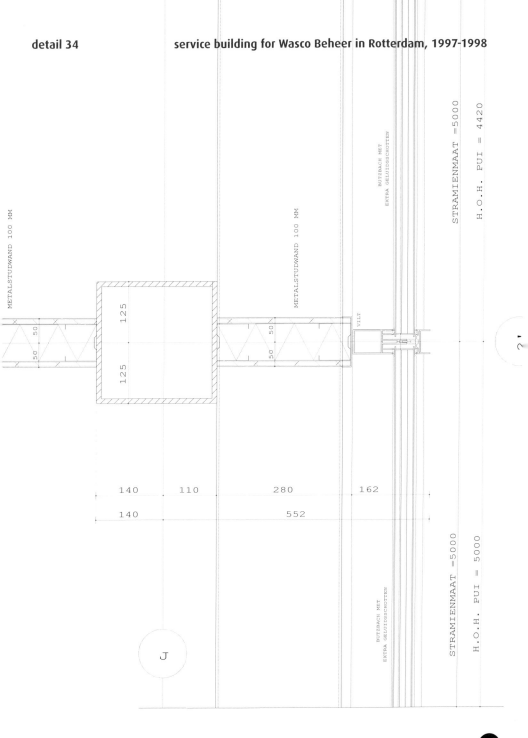

10 October 2003 Dear Tim, how far do you have to go to build something whose value is apparent to everyone except the users themselves? Can you saddle your clients with something they find beautiful but cannot open their heart to? It is like forcing a white family to adopt a black child, or as though you gave someone an unwanted birthday present which he only retrieves from the dark recesses of the cupboard when you pay a visit.

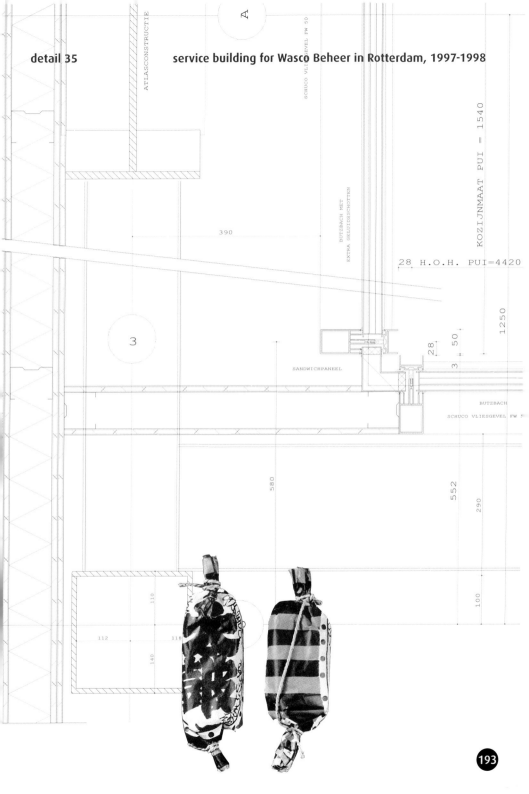

ATLASCONSTRUCTIE

A

SCHUCO VLIESGEVEL FW 50

390

BUTZBACH MET
EXTRA GELUIDSSCHOTTEN

KOZIJNMAAT PUI = 1540

28 H.O.H. PUI=4420

1250

50

28

3

3

SANDWICHPANEEL

BUTZBACH
SCHUCO VLIESGEVEL FW 5

580

552

290

110

100

112   118

140

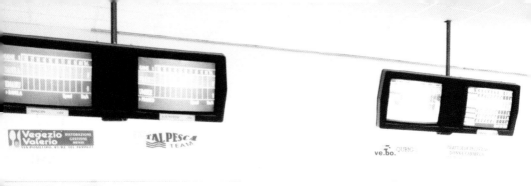

THE MORAL OF THE OBJECTS >

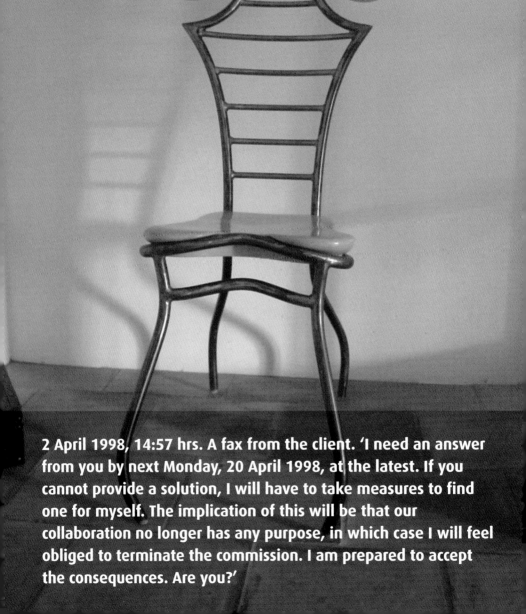

2 April 1998, 14:57 hrs. A fax from the client. 'I need an answer from you by next Monday, 20 April 1998, at the latest. If you cannot provide a solution, I will have to take measures to find one for myself. The implication of this will be that our collaboration no longer has any purpose, in which case I will feel obliged to terminate the commission. I am prepared to accept the consequences. Are you?'

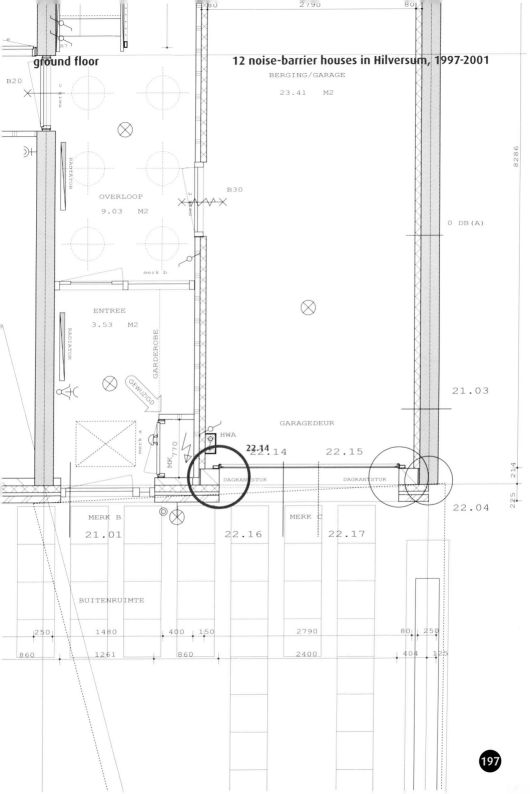

12 noise-barrier houses in Hilversum, 1997-2001

BERGING/GARAGE

23.41   M2

B20

OVERLOOP

9.03   M2

B30

ENTREE

3.53   M2

GARDEROBE

GEWIJZIGD

merk b

merk a

RADIATOR

RADIATOR

GARAGEDEUR

MK 770

HWA

22.14   22.14   22.15

DAGKANTSTUK   DAGKANTSTUK

22.04

MERK B   MERK C

21.01   22.16   22.17

BUITENRUIMTE

250   1480   400   150   2790   80   250

860   1261   860   2400   404   125

0 DB(A)

21.03

2790   80

8286

214   225

No. 01 Luijcx & Van Meegen. Owing to delays in the construction of the noise-barrier houses, they have decided to make their originally temporary rented home permanent. It is a cottage in picturesque surroundings in the woodlands of Niersen. A greater contrast than between this home, with the brook of pure, drinkable water babbling nearby, and their brawny modern house in Hilversum, would be hard to imagine.

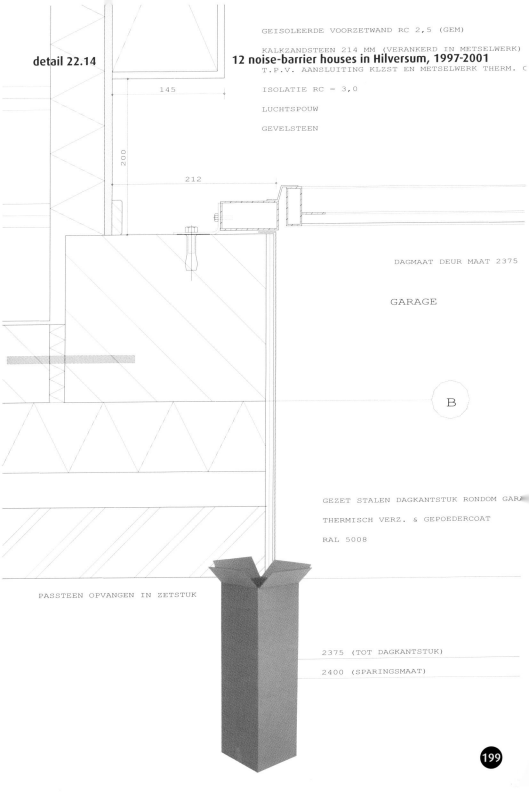

detail 22.14

12 noise-barrier houses in Hilversum, 1997-2001

GEISOLEERDE VOORZETWAND RC 2,5 (GEM)

KALKZANDSTEEN 214 MM (VERANKERD IN METSELWERK)

T.P.V. AANSLUITING KLZST EN METSELWERK THERM. C

ISOLATIE RC = 3,0

LUCHTSPOUW

GEVELSTEEN

145

200

212

DAGMAAT DEUR MAAT 2375

GARAGE

B

GEZET STALEN DAGKANTSTUK RONDOM GAR

THERMISCH VERZ. & GEPOEDERCOAT

RAL 5008

PASSTEEN OPVANGEN IN ZETSTUK

2375 (TOT DAGKANTSTUK)

2400 (SPARINGSMAAT)

No. 01 Luijcx & Van Meegen. 'How can the human longing for immaterial qualities, for sensory experiences that give rise to meaning, be met? By things. By direct, physical contact with concrete, tangible things. That is how we give purpose and meaning to the world. We are fond of things, especially of things that are capable of being cherished and of absorbing secrets.' (Louise Schouwenberg, For the Love of Things)

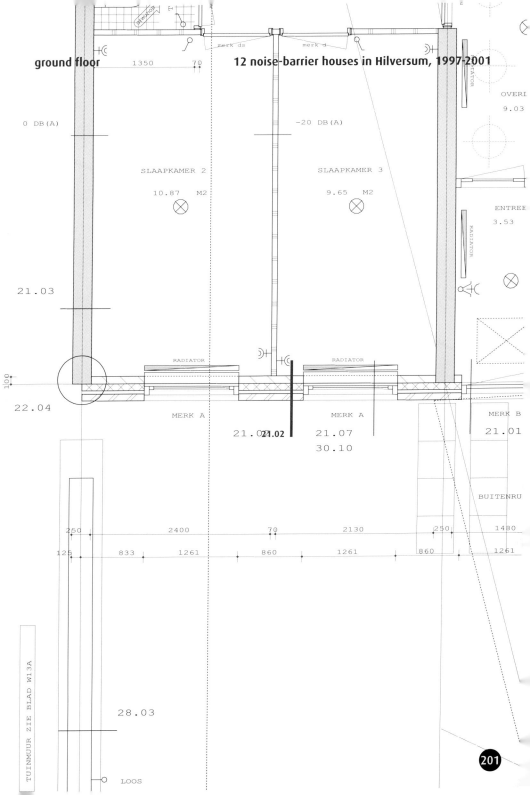

ground floor

12 noise-barrier houses in Hilversum, 1997-2001

ground floor   1350   70

OVERI
9.03

0 DB(A)

−20 DB(A)

ENTREE
3.53

SLAAPKAMER 2

10.87   M2

SLAAPKAMER 3

9.65   M2

21.03

100

22.04

RADIATOR

RADIATOR

MERK A

MERK A

MERK B

21.02 21.02

21.07

21.01

30.10

BUITENRU

250   2400   70   2130   250   1480

125   833   1261   860   1261   860   1261

TUINMUUR ZIE BLAD W13A

28.03

LOOS

6 April 1998 19:35 hrs. A fax to the client. 'In response to your request, we have selected five alternatives for the facade cladding for the noise-barrier houses. Each of these cladding materials has its own character and cost aspects. Enamelled hardened glass from Sainte Roche, Armalith panels from Leikon, Ornimat panels from SVK, Eterntile panels from Eternit and Glasal panels from Eternit. Please phone me tomorrow.'

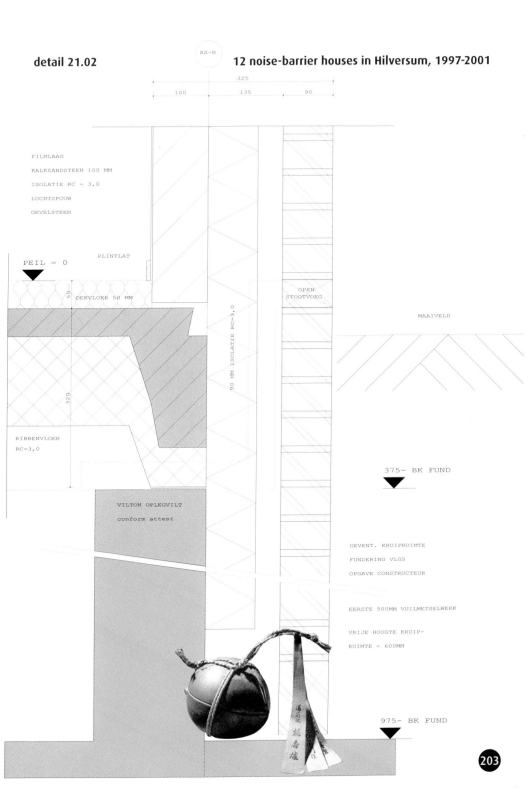

detail 21.02

AS-B

325

100   135   90

FILMLAAG

KALKZANDSTEEN 100 MM

ISOLATIE RC = 3,0

LUCHTSPOUW

GEVELSTEEN

PLINTLAT

PEIL = 0

DEKVLOER 50 MM

OPEN
STOOTVOEG

MAAIVELD

90 MM ISOLATIE RC-3,0

RIBBENVLOER
RC=3,0

375- BK FUND

VILTON OPLEGVILT

conform attest

GEVENT. KRUIPRUIMTE

FUNDERING VLGS

OPGAVE CONSTRUCTEUR

EERSTE 500MM VUILMETSELWERK

VRIJE HOOGTE KRUIP-

RUIMTE = 600MM

975- BK FUND

No. 02 Natte & Harms. They too have decided to stay in their semi-temporary, idyllically-situated holiday home. It's beginning to look like a trend: you either go for a high-tech home practically without any garden, or for a high-tech garden with a sprinkler system and a fountain but practically no house. The house is in this case secondary and is not even big enough to accommodate their grand piano. The instrument is up for sale.

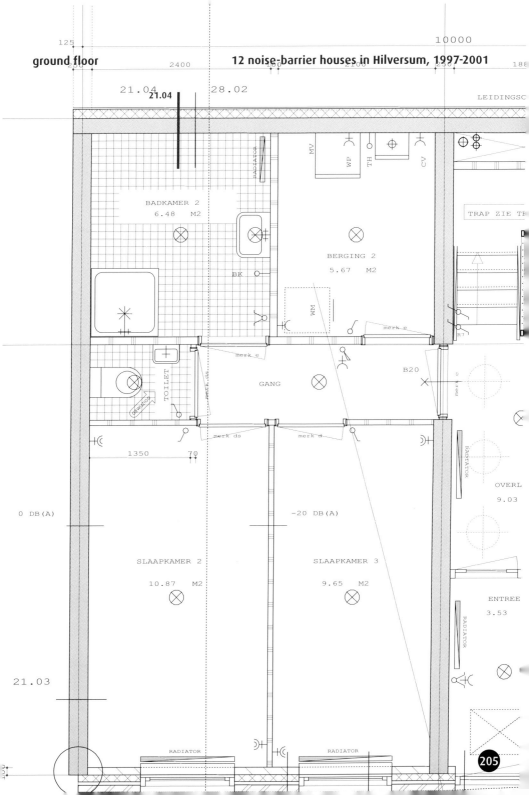

8 April 1998, 11:44 hrs. A fax from the client. 'We feel you have failed to understand what we were trying to convey in our communication of 31 March 1998. What we wish to hear from you is either a statement that you agree with our preference for brickwork facades, or a statement that you wish to hand the commission back to us. Unless we hear from you by Thursday, we will start seeking another architect.'

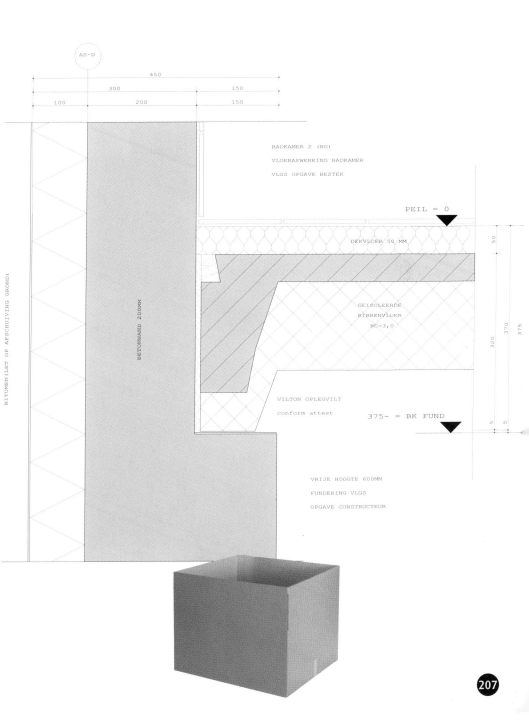

AS-D

450

300   150

100   200   150

BITUMEN (LET OP AFSCHUIVING GROND)

BETONWAND 200MM

BADKAMER 2 (BG)

VLOERAFWERKING BADKAMER

VLGS OPGAVE BESTEK

PEIL = 0

DEKVLOER 50 MM

50

GEISOLEERDE
RIBBENVLOER
RC=3,0

370

375

320

VILTON OPLEGVILT

conform attest   375- = BK FUND

5 5

VRIJE HOOGTE 600MM

FUNDERING VLGS

OPGAVE CONSTRUCTEUR

No. 03 Medema & Olislagers. Another couple in a temporary dwelling, but unlike 01 and 02 they are going to move into the new noise-barrier house. Apart from a chair and a piano, there are few possession they care enough about to take with them. Their most cherished item is their eleven-month old daughter, but she is asleep. Instead of photographing her, we take a photo of a toy piano.

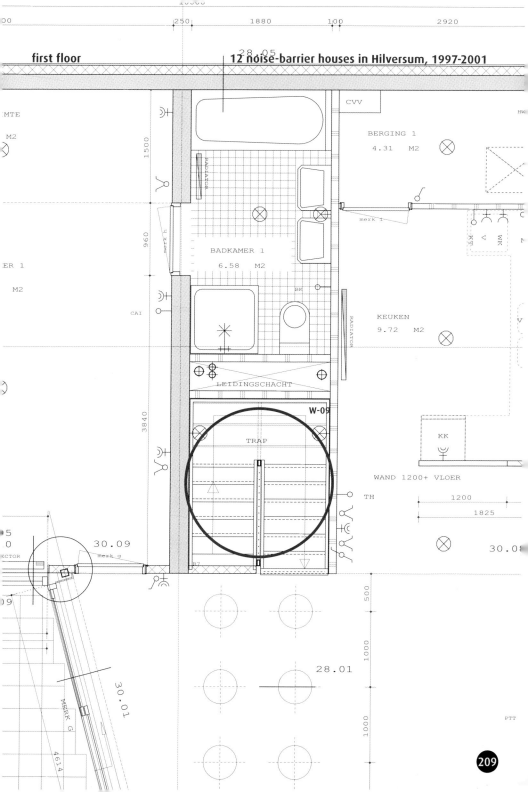

CVV

BERGING 1
4.31 M2

merk i

BADKAMER 1
6.58 M2

BK

KEUKEN
9.72 M2

RADIATOR

LEIDINGSCHACHT

W-09

TRAP

KK

WAND 1200+ VLOER

TH

1200

1825

30.09

30.0

merk g

30.01

28.01

MERK G

4614

PTT

9 April 1998, 20:12 hrs. A fax to the client. 'We can design a brick-built house, of course, but the present form of the sound barrier houses is not suited to that material. The best idea, in our view, is to get together with the Municipality of Hilversum and explain that the design starting points have changed, before we invest effort, time and money on another design. Please phone us rather than faxing.'

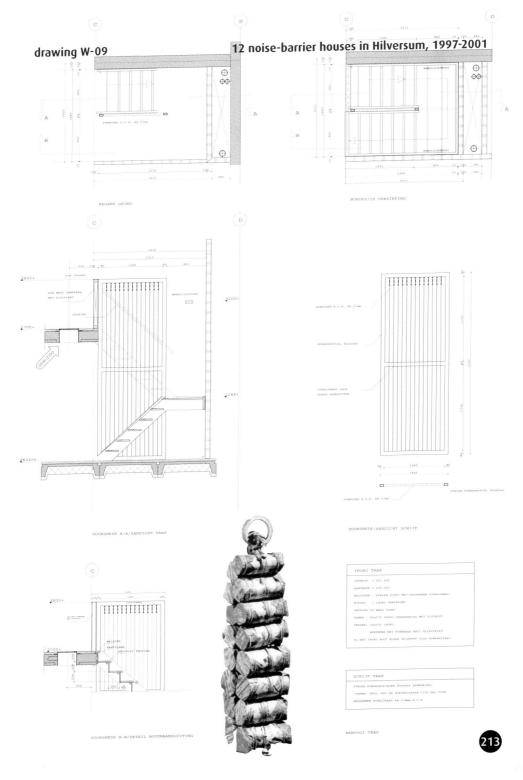

BEGANE GROND

BORDES/1E VERDIEPING

DOORSNEDE A-A/AANZICHT TRAP

DOORSNEDE/AANZICHT SCHIJF

IROKO TRAP

SCHIJF TRAP

DOORSNEDE B-B/DETAIL BOVENAANSLUITING

RENVOOI TRAP

No. 04 Groenendijk & Mijailovic. Living in Amstelveen, they were originally one of 358 candidates for 38 houses. 'You've no right to complain,' said the contractor, then still cocksure. They left Amstelveen because of the closeness of Schiphol Airport and the lack of a forest. Both failings are now resolved in the Hilversum location. The noise-barrier dwellings are perfect in their eyes, apart from the lack of a conservatory.

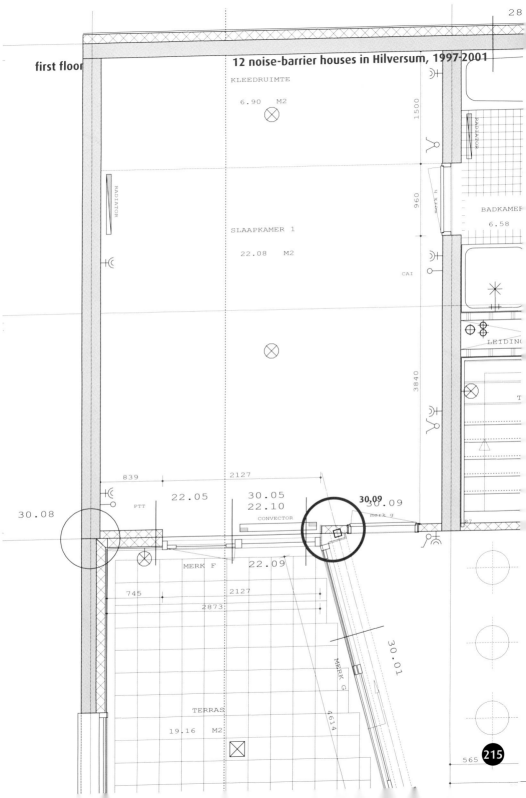

12 noise-barrier houses in Hilversum, 1997-2001

28

KLEEDRUIMTE

6.90   M2

1500

BADKAMER

6.58

960

SLAAPKAMER 1

22.08   M2

RADIATOR

RADIATOR

CAI

LEIDING

3840

T

839   2127

22.05   30.05
            22.10

PTT   CONVECTOR

30,09 30.09

merk g

30.08

MERK F   22.09

745   2127

2873

30·01

MERK G

4614

TERRAS

19.16   M2

565 **215**

No. 04 Groenendijk & Mijailovic. A chair in their bedroom. How
will it look in the new house? And where will they put it? Does it
matter? Do household effects determine the character of the
home, or does the house determine the arrangement of
household effects? More importantly, do the occupants
determine the household effects, or do the household effects
determine the character of the occupants? The latter, I suspect.

12 noise-barrier houses in Hilversum, 1997-2001

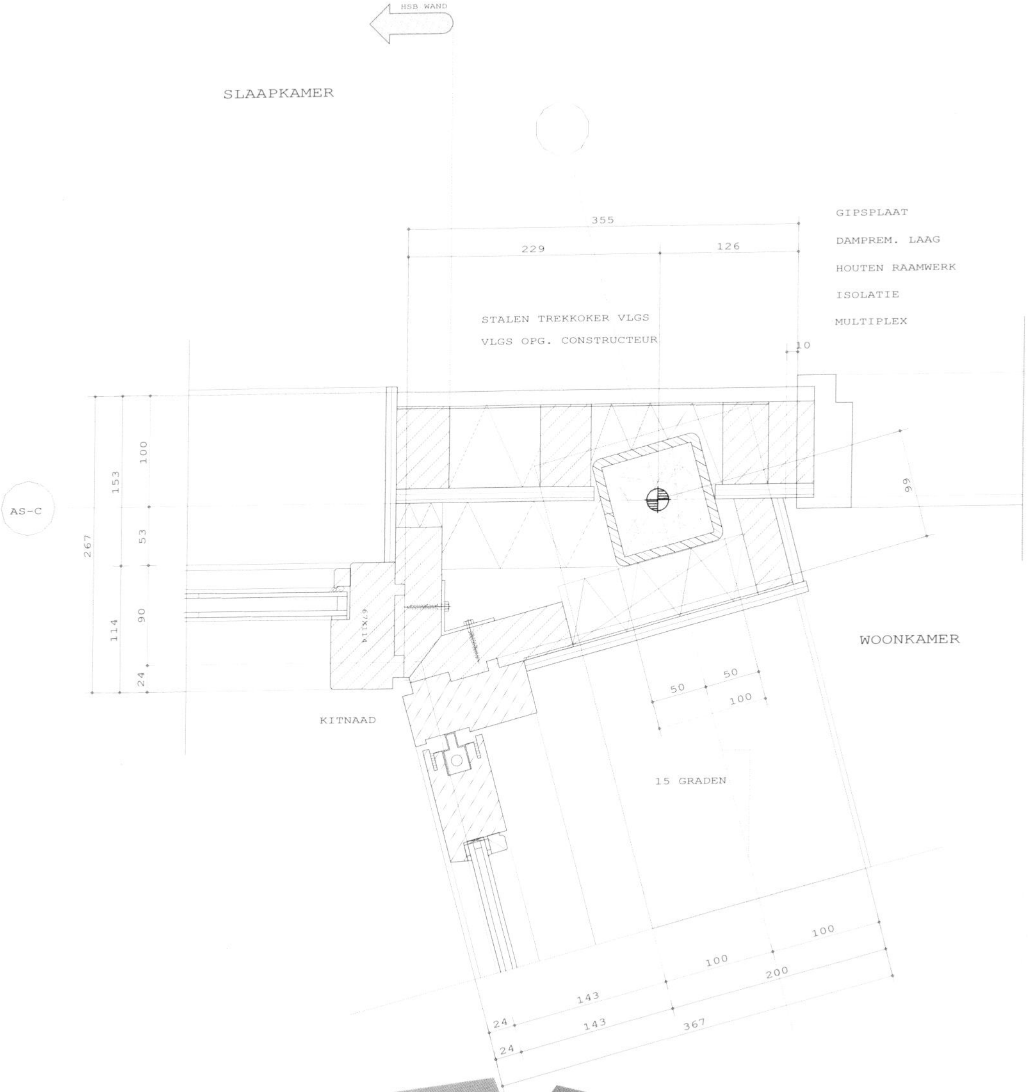
HSB WAND
SLAAPKAMER
355
229
126
GIPSPLAAT
DAMPREM. LAAG
HOUTEN RAAMWERK
ISOLATIE
MULTIPLEX
STALEN TREKKOKER VLGS
VLGS OPG. CONSTRUCTEUR
10
AS-C
267
153
100
53
114
90
24
99
67X114
WOONKAMER
KITNAAD
50
50
100
15 GRADEN
100
100
200
143
143
367
24
24

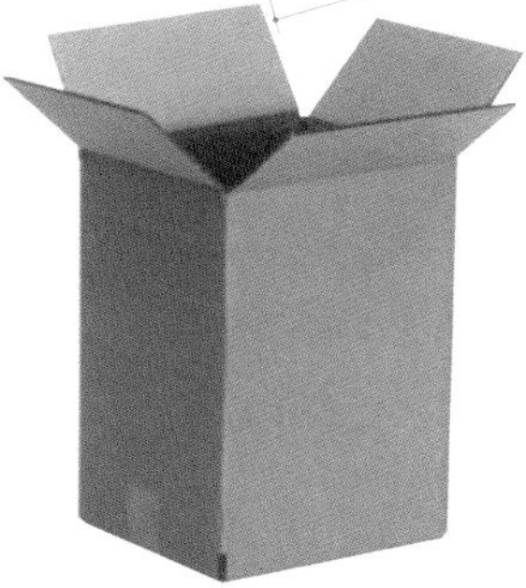

14 April 1998, 07:31 hrs. A fax from the client. 'I have just read your fax of Thursday. It will surely be clear to you that we are the client, and as such neither you nor we ought to approach the Municipality before more clarity has been obtained. Consultation is indeed necessary, but there has to be something to consult about. From that point of view, we should not be thinking about consulting with them but about informing them.'

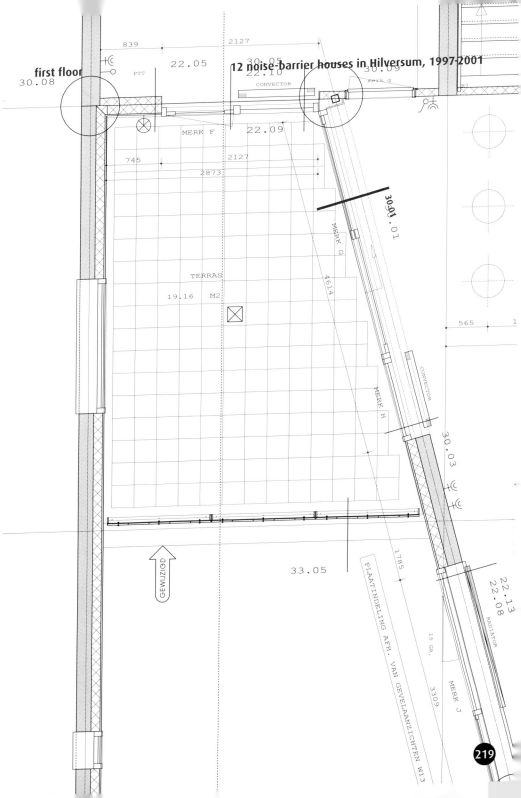

first floor
30.08

839   2127   22.05   30.05   12 noise-barrier houses in Hilversum, 1997-2001   30.09

PTT   22.10   CONVECTOR   merk g

MERK F   22.09

745   2127   30.01 · 01

2873

MERK G

TERRAS   4614

19.16   M2

CONVECTOR

MERK H

565   1

30.03

GEWIJZIGD

33.05   1785   22.13
                          22.08

PLAATINDELING AFH. VAN GEVELAANZICHTEN W13   RADIATOR

15 GR.   3309   MERK J

219

No. 05 Camfferman & Mijailovic. At the start of our visit, we took some snaps of their two little darlings' toys, which are generously scattered around the house. A little later, we were allowed to inspect the contents of their cupboards and photograph their treasured possessions. It's bizarre what people keep and collect. What could make anyone want to collect a boxful of old clay pipes? How often do they look at the things?

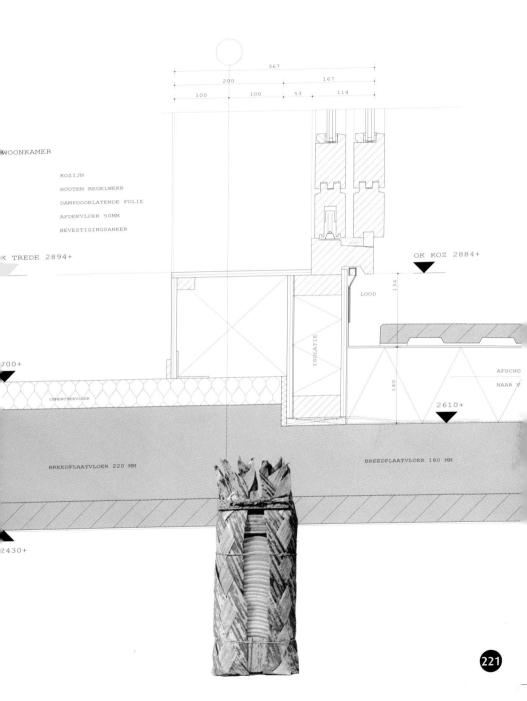

WOONKAMER

KOZIJN
HOUTEN REGELWERK
DAMPDOORLATENDE FOLIE
AFDEKVLOER 50MM
BEVESTIGINGSANKER

K TREDE 2894+

OK KOZ 2884+

LOOD

ISOLATIE

700+

CEMENTDEKVLOER

AFSCHO
NAAR V

2610+

BREEDPLAATVLOER 220 MM

BREEDPLAATVLOER 180 MM

2430+

367
200
100   100   53   114
167
134
140

No. 05 Camfferman & Mijailovic. What is the difference between a passion for collecting and mere possessiveness? Perhaps they are two faces of the same mania. Both stand for a fear of losing what is singular. Nobody wants to throw away something potentially of sentimental value. Suppose you discard something but later realize it was your favourite thing. Terrible. That thought alone justifies having as many boxrooms as possible.

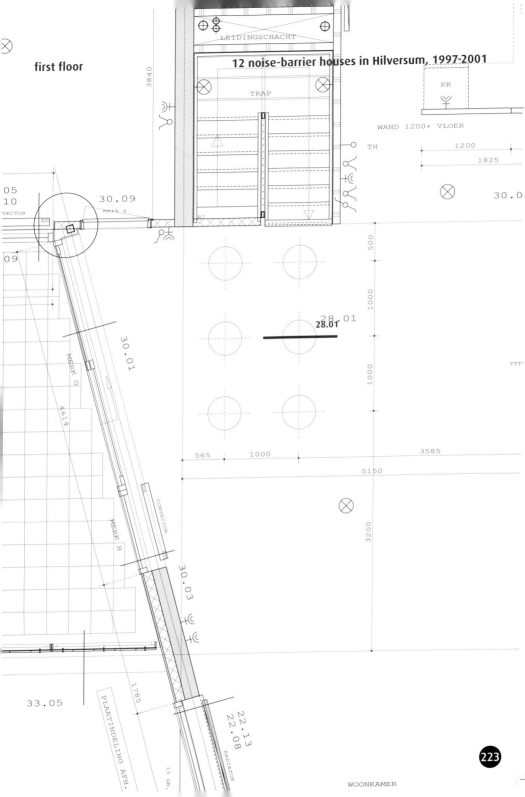

first floor

12 noise-barrier houses in Hilversum, 1997-2001

LEIDINGSCHACHT

TRAP

KK

WAND 1200+ VLOER

1200

1825

TH

3840

30.09

merk g

VECTOR

05
10

09

30.01

MERK G

4614

CONVECTOR

MERK H

30.03

33.05

1785

PLAATINDELING AFH.

15 GR.

RADIATOR

22.13
22.08

500

1000

1000

28.01

565   1000

3585

5150

3200

PTT

WOONKAMER

19 July 2002, 20:17 hrs. A fax to the client. 'With the harbour in sight, we can only conclude that now, during the fitting-out stage, many things are being finished off without the previous passion being there. To mention a few examples: garage door too low, balcony parapet too thin, front facade cladding incorrectly mounted, wrong colour plumbing on the roof, black concrete footing absent from garden walls...'

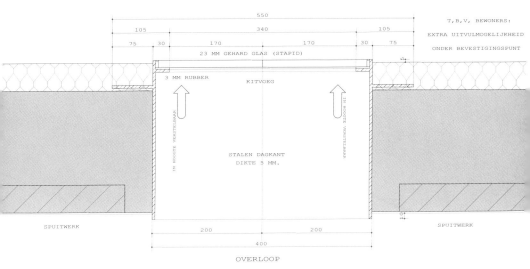

WOONKAMER

T,B,V, BEWONERS:
EXTRA UITVULMOGELIJKHEID
ONDER BEVESTIGINGSPUNT

23 MM GEHARD GLAS (STAPID)
3 MM RUBBER   KITVOEG
STALEN DAGKANT
DIKTE 5 MM.

SPUITWERK   SPUITWERK

OVERLOOP

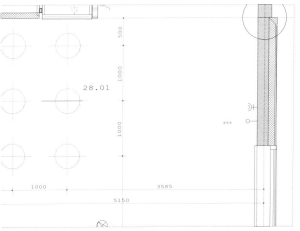

28.01

CYLINDERS VERDIEPINGSVLOER
HART 1E CYLINDER VERT. 500MM UIT AS C 2E EN 3E H
HART 1E CYLINDER HOR. 3585MM UIT AS 7 H.O.H. 100(

ZIE FRAGMENT

No. 06 Nagtegaal & Tinga. Dick Nagtegaal lives in a holiday chalet in Loosdrecht. Esther Tinga lives in a house in Koekoeklaan, Bussum. Dick moved in with Esther a year ago. All he had with him was his laptop computer. Recently, he bought a supersonic hifi complete with headphones. If someone is prepared to make him an acceptable offer, Dick is prepared to sell his noise-barrier house, number 06.

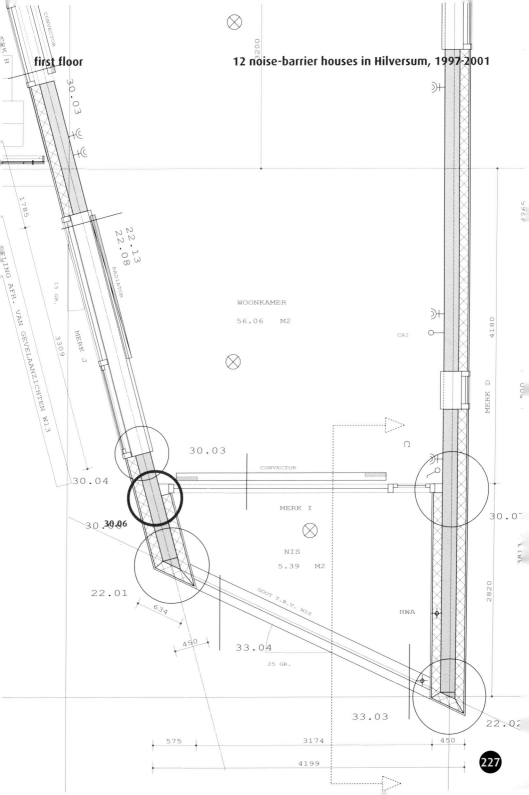

30.03

22.13
22.08
RADIATOR

WOONKAMER

56.06   M2

CAI

30.03

CONVECTOR

MERK I

NIS

5.39   M2

22.01

30.04

30.06   30.06

634

450

33.04

25 GR.

GOOT T.B.V. NIS

HWA

33.03

22.0?

575

3174

450

4199

MERK J

3309

15 GR.

1785

AFH. VAN GEVELAANZICHTEN W13

3200

MERK D

4180

30.0?

2820

3813

CONVECTOR

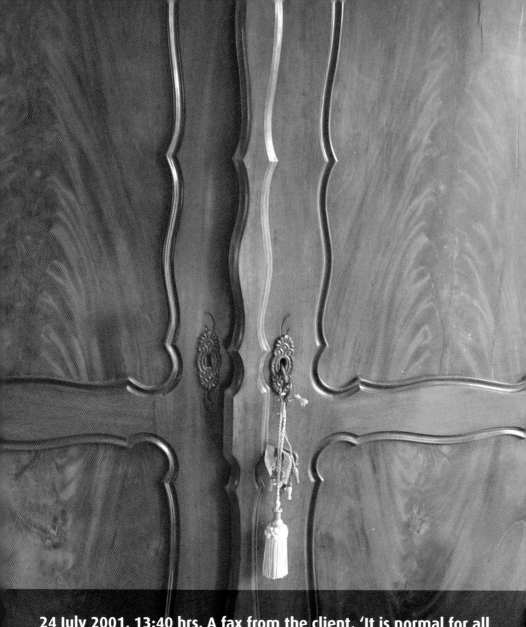

24 July 2001, 13:40 hrs. A fax from the client. 'It is normal for all the defects to appear at the same time, at completion. Although we have invested considerable time and effort in the preparation and supervision, it remains human handiwork. You cannot expect other people to see it through the same eyes as you when you look at the work, whether with regard to purchaser guidance, project preparation or execution.'

12 noise-barrier houses in Hilversum, 1997-2001

HOUTEN REGELWERK

ISOLATIE RC - 3,0

WATERKERENDE FOLIE

SPOUW (MATIG VENTILEREN)

TRESPA M51.0.1 SATIN

BEVESTIGING VLGS

OPGAVE LEVERANCIER

AANSLUITING ZIE
DET. NR. 30.04

MULTIPLEX

DAMPREMMENDE LAAG

HOUTEN RAAMWERK

FOLIE

ISOLATIEPLAAT

BEVESTIGINGSANKER

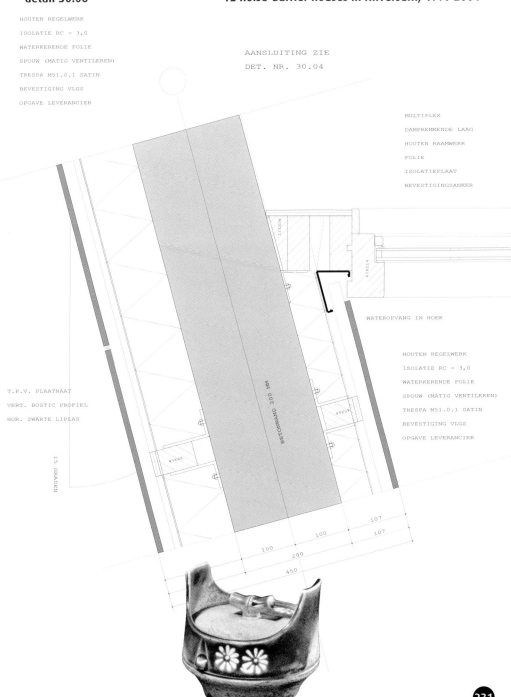

WATEROPVANG IN HOEK

HOUTEN REGELWERK

ISOLATIE RC - 3,0

WATERKERENDE FOLIE

SPOUW (MATIG VENTILEREN)

TRESPA M51.0.1 SATIN

BEVESTIGING VLGS

OPGAVE LEVERANCIER

T.P.V. PLAATNAAT

VERT. BOSTIC PROFIEL

HOR. ZWARTE LIPLAS

15 GRADEN

BETONWAND 200 MM

45X68

45X68

107
107

100
100

100

200

450

No. 07 Verwoerd & Meevis. They used to live in De Rading, and before that in a flat. Then they had a house in Lage Vuurscheweg. Next, they lived three years in Abel Tasmanstraat, then for eighteen months in Vosmaerlaan and finally another eighteen months in Birkenheuvelweg. They bought a sofa and an ornamental fireplace. They junk everything every time they move house, except the chandelier and that antique cupboard.

west facade & section AA

12 noise-barrier houses in Hilversum, 1997-2001

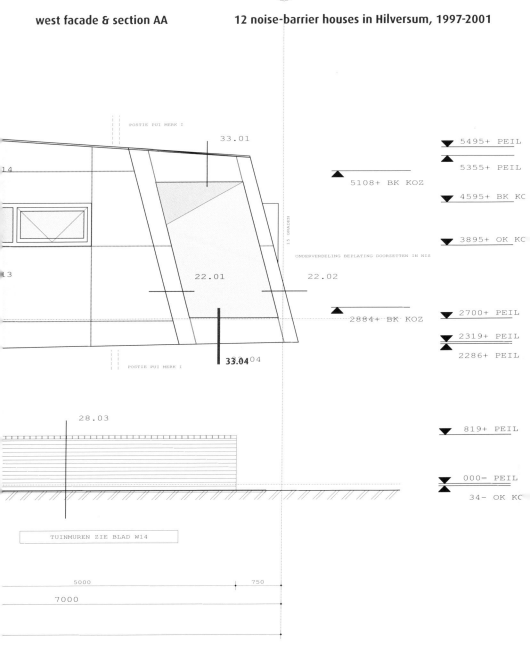

22 August 2001. A letter to the client. 'Naturally we understand that some basic assumptions inevitably have to be revised during the construction process. Something we find hard to accept, however, is that various things are now going awry despite our meticulous care all the way from the initial sketch to implementation. We trust that the points we have identified will be properly remedied.'

NIS

DAKBEDEKKING DOORZETTEN IN GOOT
THERM. ONDERBREKING

AFSCHOT

150   125

ALUMINIUM AFDEKKER

2719+

VENTILATIE

2650+

60

15 GRADEN

MM

2430

VENTILATIE   2319

DAMPREMMENDE LAAG

HOUTEN REGELWERK

500   ISOLATIE RC = 3,0

WATERKERENDE FOLIE

SPOUW (MATIG VENTILEREN)

WBP-MULTIPLEX PANELEN ZILVERKLEURIG

- KLEUR GELIJKWAARDIG AAN TRESPA M51.0.1 SATIN

BEVESTIGING VLGS

OPGAVE LEVERANCIER

IJDE OVERSTEK

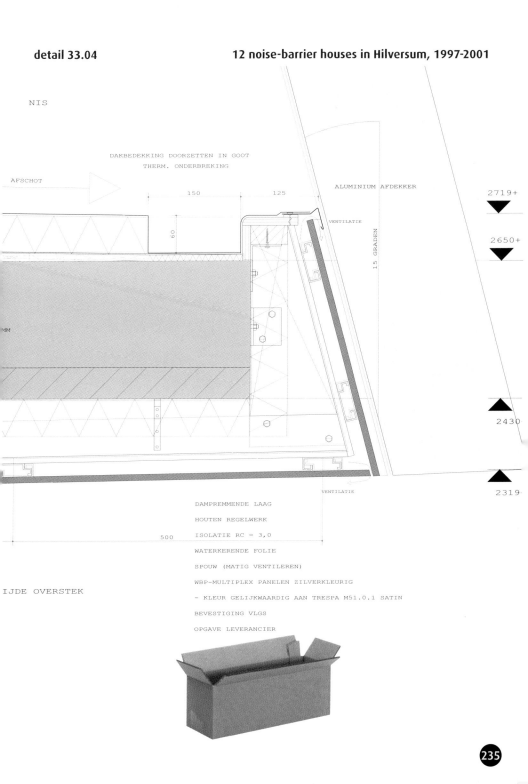

235

No. 08 Jenster. He has collected ideas for the interior design of his new home in a kind of sample book of atmospheric examples. The kitchen and the terrace, the living room and the bedrooms, the front garden and the garage: all these are beautifully matched and balanced. None of the furnishings have been ordered yet, but once chosen the atmosphere can be delivered within two months.

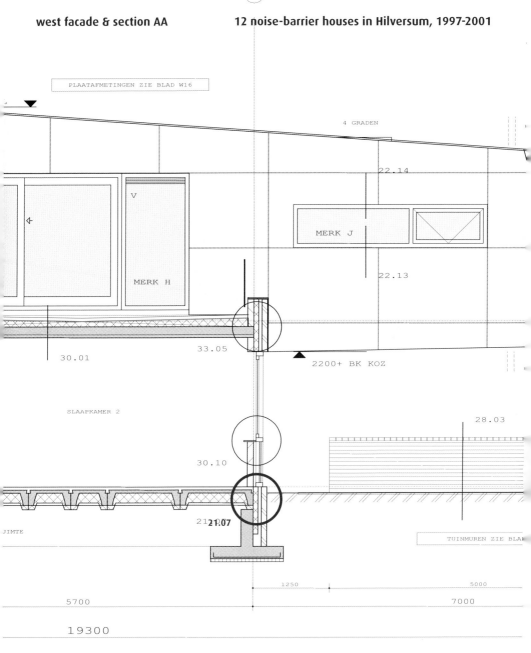

PLAATAFMETINGEN ZIE BLAD W16

4 GRADEN

22.14

V

MERK J

MERK H

22.13

30.01

33.05

2200+ BK KOZ

SLAAPKAMER 2

28.03

30.10

21.07

JIMTE

TUINMUREN ZIE BLAI

1250

5000

5700

7000

19300

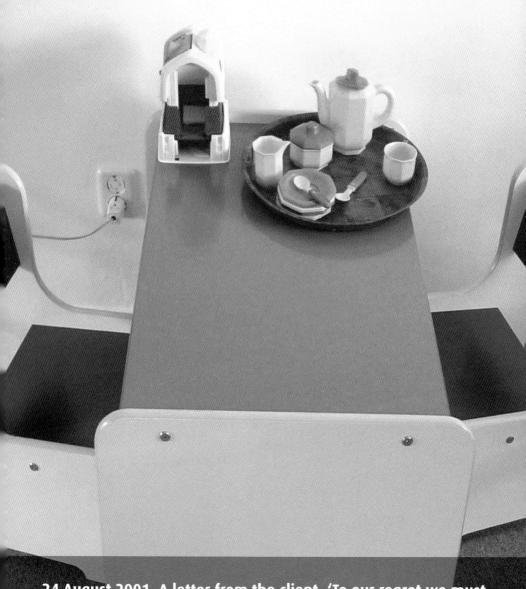

24 August 2001. A letter from the client. 'To our regret we must agree with you that not all components comply exactly with the working drawings. However, as already noted, it is normal for defects to become apparent during the construction process. We appreciated your efforts in supervising the project during the construction process too, which made it possible for us to tackle such matters together.'

detail 21.07

12 noise-barrier houses in Hilversum, 1997-2001

325

100 155 70

100 41 114 70

FILMLAAG

KALKZANDSTEEN 100 MM

ISOLATIE 70 MM

FOLIE

LUCHTSPOUW

KOZIJN

EMALIT AAN BUITENZIJDE

PLINTLAT

PEIL = 0

DEKVLOER 50 MM

50

34- = OK KOZIJN

MAAIVELD

RIBBENVLOER
RC=3,0

370

320

PREFAB KANTPLANK
50X250 MM

20

375- BK FUND

VILTON OPLEGVILT

conform attest

MM ISOLATIE RC=3,0

GEVENT. KRUIPRUIMTE

FUNDERING VLGS

OPGAVE CONSTRUCTEUR

EERSTE 500MM VUILMETSELWERK

VRIJE HOOGTE KRUIP-

RUIMTE = 600MM

975- BK FUND

No. 09 Wijnberg & Wickel. All they are taking with them is that intrepid motorbike, for scrambling in the woods around Hilversum. That and two inoffensive toddler chairs and a poisonous green table. They are leaving the rest behind them. They are glad to be leaving the polders. Goodbye boring old suburbs. Their new house is like the motorbike – ideal for scrambling in the wilderness of new housing estate.

west facade & section AA 12 noise-barrier houses in Hilversum, 1997-2001

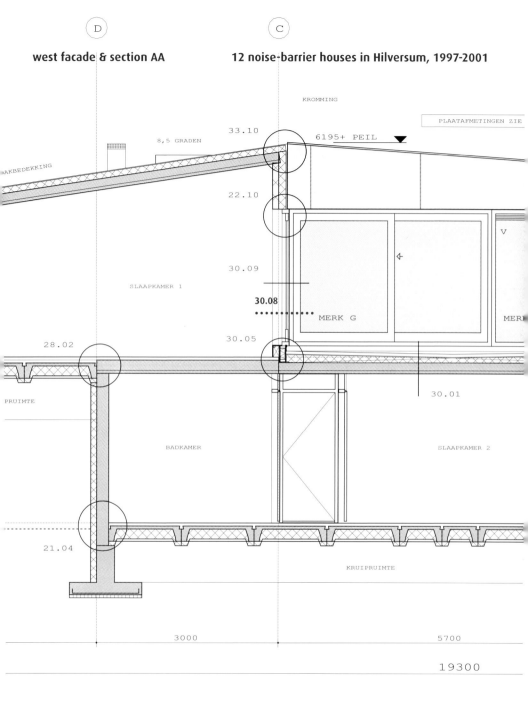

KROMMING

PLAATAFMETINGEN ZIE

33.10

8,5 GRADEN

6195+ PEIL ▼

AKBEDEKKING

22.10

30.09

V

SLAAPKAMER 1

30.08
•••••••••••• MERK G   MERK

30.05

28.02

30.01

PRUIMTE

BADKAMER

SLAAPKAMER 2

21.04

KRUIPRUIMTE

3000   5700

19300

(165)

5 September 2001. A letter to the client. 'During the whole construction stage, the team has been doing its utmost to make sure things run smoothly. We believe we were successful in this until a short while ago. It is only logical that solutions have to be found during the building process which deviate from our drawings. The points we have raised, however, are differences that fall outside the limits.'

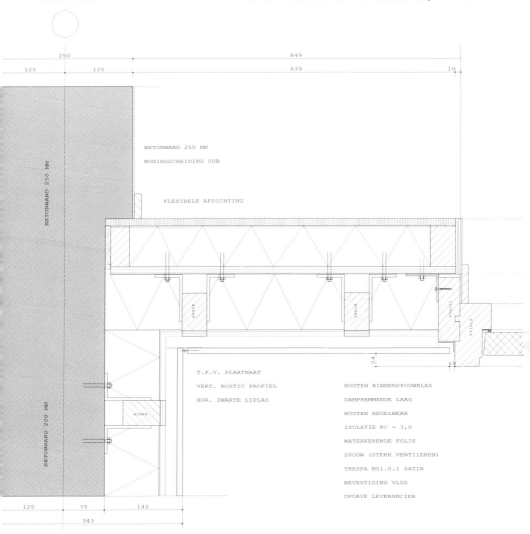

BETONWAND 250 MM

WONINGSCHEIDING 0DB

FLEXIBELE AFDICHTING

BETONWAND 250 MM

BETONWAND 200 MM

T.P.V. PLAATNAAT

VERT. BOSTIC PROFIEL

HOR. ZWARTE LIPLAS

45X68

45X68

40x113

47X114

HOUTEN BINNENSPOUWBLAD

DAMPREMMENDE LAAG

HOUTEN REGELWERK

ISOLATIE RC = 3,0

WATERKERENDE FOLIE

SPOUW (STERK VENTILEREN)

TRESPA M51.0.1 SATIN

BEVESTIGING VLGS

OPGAVE LEVERANCIER

250 849 125 125 839 10

125 75 143 343 24 10

No. 10 Salomons & Neysen. The wall of the entrance hall will be studded with photos of their children and relatives. The centrepiece will be a picture of their old house, built in 1936, in Orionlaan, Hilversum. A reproduction of a painting of a horseman in a red jacket, holding a whip, will hang on their living room wall. A glass bowl elsewhere in the living room will hold artificial fruit – odourless and undecaying.

south facade   **12 noise-barrier houses in Hilversum, 1997-2001**

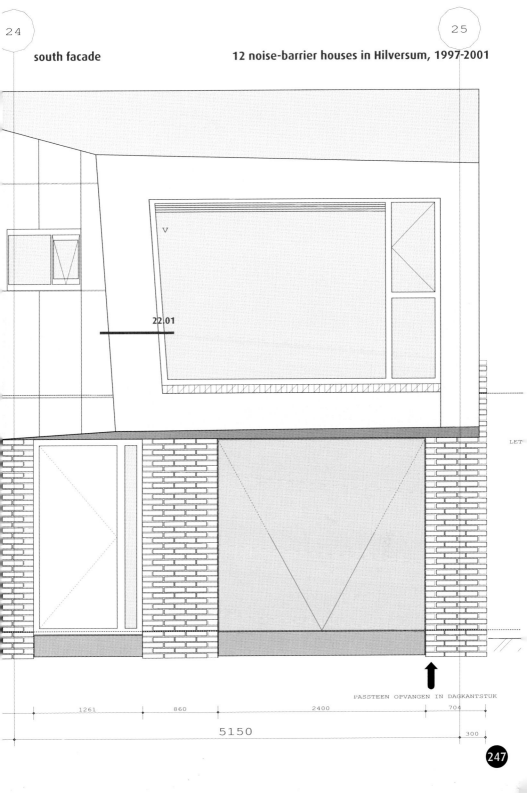

V

22.01

LET

PASSTEEN OPVANGEN IN DAGKANTSTUK

| 1261 | 860 | 2400 | 704 |

5150

300

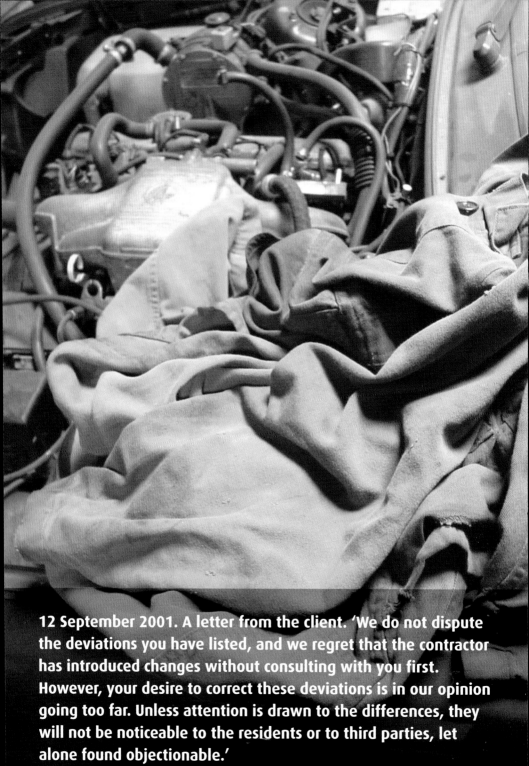

12 September 2001. A letter from the client. 'We do not dispute the deviations you have listed, and we regret that the contractor has introduced changes without consulting with you first. However, your desire to correct these deviations is in our opinion going too far. Unless attention is drawn to the differences, they will not be noticeable to the residents or to third parties, let alone found objectionable.'

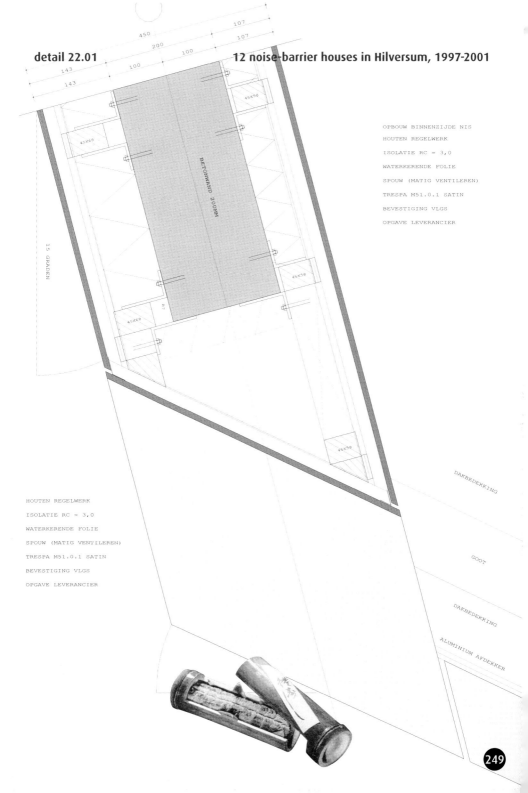

450
107
200
100
107
100
143
143

45X50
45X60

BETONWAND 200MM

15 GRADEN

47

45X60
45X50
45X50

OPBOUW BINNENZIJDE NIS
HOUTEN REGELWERK
ISOLATIE RC = 3,0
WATERKERENDE FOLIE
SPOUW (MATIG VENTILEREN)
TRESPA M51.0.1 SATIN
BEVESTIGING VLGS
OPGAVE LEVERANCIER

HOUTEN REGELWERK
ISOLATIE RC = 3,0
WATERKERENDE FOLIE
SPOUW (MATIG VENTILEREN)
TRESPA M51.0.1 SATIN
BEVESTIGING VLGS
OPGAVE LEVERANCIER

DAKBEDEKKING

GOOT

DAKBEDEKKING

ALUMINIUM AFDEKKER

No. 11 Hunting. A rather remarkable meeting, not at his home but at his place of work. But what do you mean, work? Perhaps this little garage was actually his home and the new, large house was a matter of necessity; or at best something he could no longer get out of, because we had seduced him for some mysterious reason. An indispensible knickknack, as he himself put it, like the dusty old Porsche in his garage.

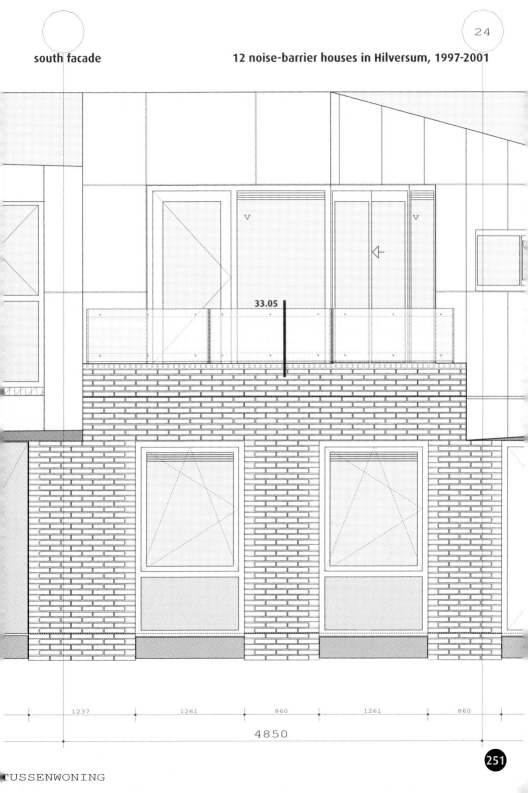

33.05

| 1237 | 1261 | 860 | 1261 | 860 |

4850

TUSSENWONING

No. 12 Del Mistro & Ulenberg. The blackest page of this book.
Apart from their toothbrushes, Del Mistro & Ulenberg did not
have a single possession in their temporary accommodation.
There was simply nothing to photograph. They had long been
looking for an apartment in Hilversum, but everything was too
expensive. Now, for half the money, they have 'an apartment
with a penthouse on the ground floor'.

detail 33.05

12 noise-barrier houses in Hilversum, 1997-2001

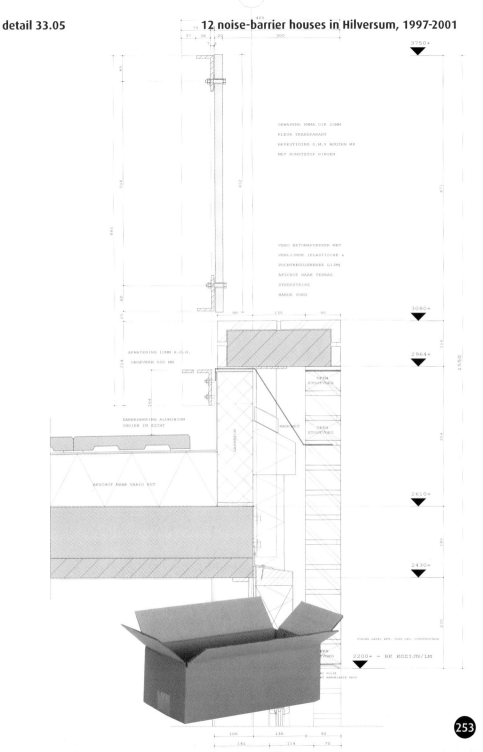

GEWAPEND PMMA DIK 20MM
KLEUR TRANSPARANT
BEVESTIGING D.M.V BOUTEN M8
MET KUNSTSTOF RINGEN

VEBO BETONAFDEKKER MET
VERLIJMDE (PLASTISCHE &
VOCHTREGULERENDE LIJM)
AFSCHOT NAAR TERRAS
STEENSTRIPS
HARDE VOEG

AFWATERING 10MM H.O.H.
ONGEVEER 500 MM

DAKBEDEKKING ALUMINIUM
INDIEN IN ZICHT

AFSCHOT NAAR VARIO PUT

OPEN STOOTVOEG

MANCHET

GALBBETON

OPEN STOOTVOEG

STALEN LATEI AFM. VLGS OPG. CONSTRUCTEUR

2200+ - BK KOZIJN/LM

3750+

3080+

2964+

2610+

2430+

AS-B

253

CREDITS >

CONCEPT   MAURICE NIO with CAROLE SCHMIT

TRANSLATION   VICTOR JOSEPH

PHOTOGRAPHY   FRANCESCO JODICE
page 2, 6, 18, 100, 136, 194, 254 & the double spreads of part one & three

                                            ROB PONSEN
                              the double spreads of part four

                                        PETER VENEMA
                                                part one

                                        AREK SEREDYN
            part two & three & the double spreads of part two

                                       CAROLE SCHMIT
                                               part four

DRAWINGS   BDG ARCHITEKTEN INGENIEURS
                                                part one

              CHRISTEL VAN DER HULST & HANS LARSEN
                                               part two

                                        REMCO ARNOLD
                                       part three & four

GRAPHIC DESIGN   MAURICE NIO

FINANCIAL SUPPORT   THE NETHERLANDS FOUNDATION
                      for visual arts, design and architecture

COPYRIGHT   AUTHOR & 010 PUBLISHERS ROTTERDAM
                                       www.010publishers.nl

ISBN   90 6450 468 7